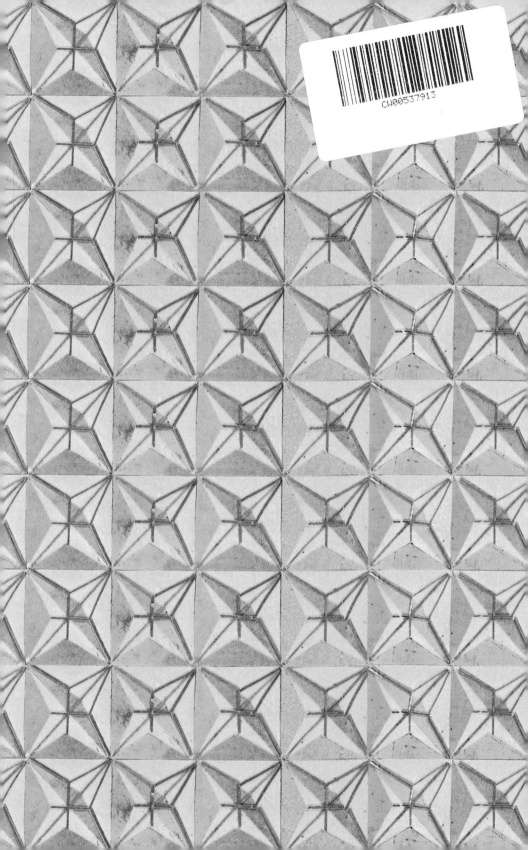

CW00537913

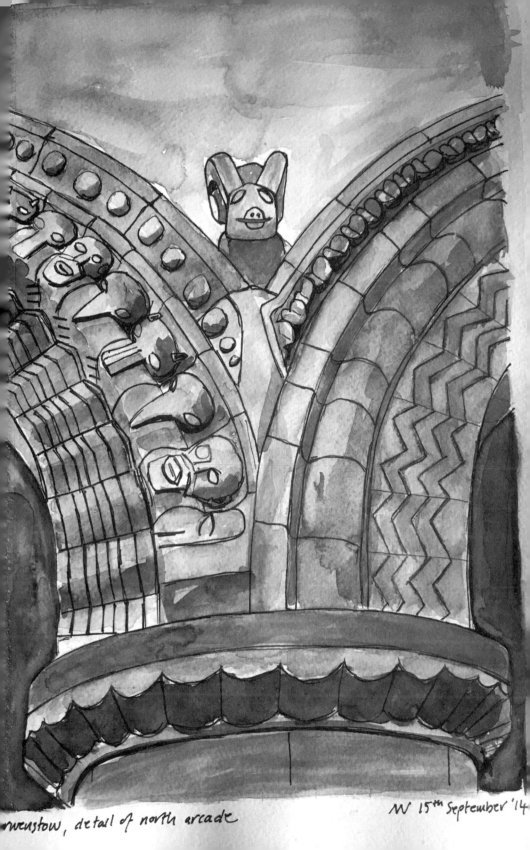

rwenstow, detail of north arcade

NN 15th September '14

Published by Little Toller Books in 2019
Lower Dairy, Toller Fratrum, Dorset

Text, photographs and sketchbooks © Alex Woodcock 2019

Typeset in Garamond by Little Toller Books

Printed by TJ International, Cornwall, Padstow

All papers used by Little Toller Books are natural, recyclable products made from wood grown in sustainable, well-managed forests

A catalogue record for this book is available from the British Library

ISBN 978-1-908213-69-3

KING

OF

DUST

ADVENTURES IN FORGOTTEN SCULPTURE

Alex Woodcock

LITTLE TOLLER BOOKS

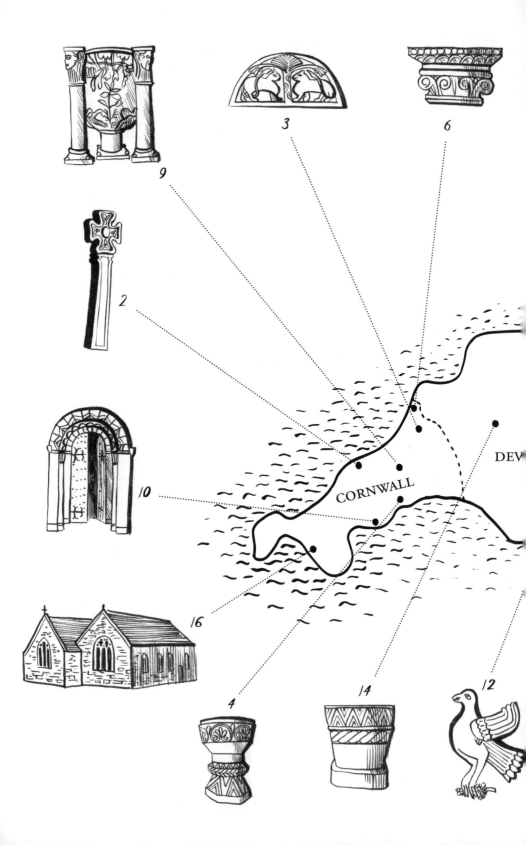

9

3

6

2

10

16

4

14

12

CORNWALL

DEV

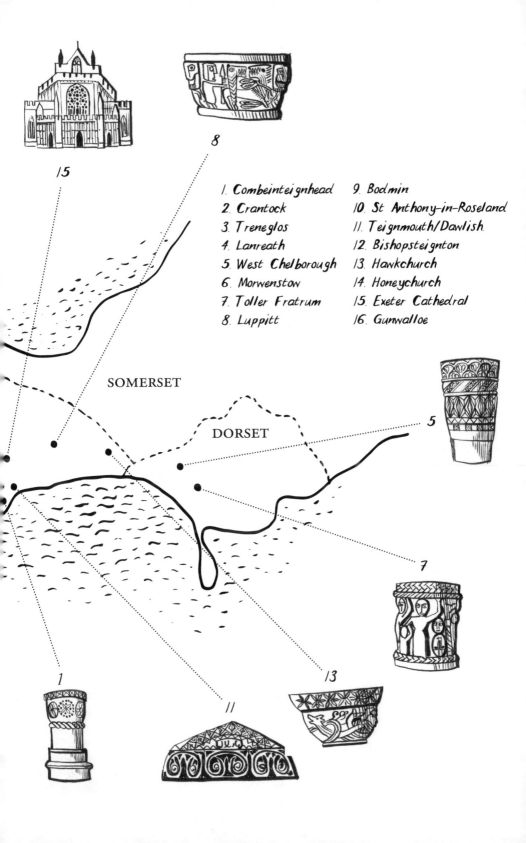

1. Combeinteignhead
2. Crantock
3. Treneglos
4. Lanreath
5. West Chelborough
6. Morwenstow
7. Toller Fratrum
8. Luppitt
9. Bodmin
10. St Anthony-in-Roseland
11. Teignmouth/Dawlish.
12. Bishopsteignton
13. Hawkchurch
14. Honeychurch
15. Exeter Cathedral
16. Gunwalloe

SOMERSET

DORSET

Contents

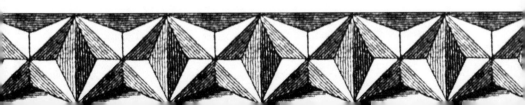

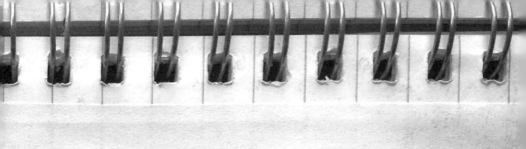

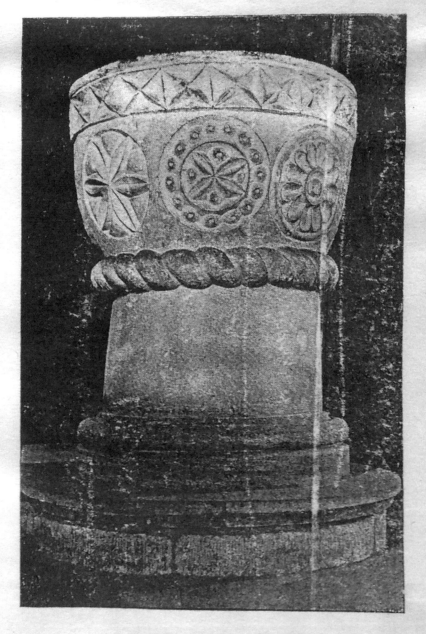

COMBE-IN-TEIGNHEAD.

Stones

A quick inventory: there is a chunk of alabaster under the table, a sizeable flint props up one end of a broken shelf and scattered on the windowsill are numerous holed stones, some rose quartz, a couple of sea-urchin fossils and a chalk pebble. Directly in front of me, on my desk, a rectangle of Caen limestone (on which I've carved three four-pointed stars) works as a bookend, and beside it is a lump of polished lapis lazuli. To weigh down loose papers I use a piece of Devon slate that the sea has worn smooth, its hard veins of white quartz standing proud. Next to my mug of tea there is a tiny pyramid of blue sodalite and a rounded piece of granite, and by my feet an irregular-shaped offcut of Portland limestone.

I am obsessed with stones. I think it's because they suggest stability and permanence, a physical connection with something ancient. Or it might be that the 'pebble of rough / and unprepossessing stone' as the poet Kenneth White puts it, when 'cut asunder / shows / a blue-gleaming layer of amethyst – / there is a principle / of beauty and order / at the heart of chaos'. Longevity, beauty, order: stone has it all. In times of uncertainty perhaps this is why it is to the landscapes and buildings of stone that I always return. To its colours, textures and patterns. To its legacy of sculpture, and more recently, to my ability to work it with a chisel. This happened almost by accident. It was an August afternoon in 2004. I had an address, a map printed out from the internet and a vague sense that I'd been to this particular town in Somerset before, though I couldn't remember when or why. Déjà vu aside, I had a more pressing problem: I was lost. The roads were unnamed, there appeared to be nobody around to ask for directions, and I was beginning to question what I had signed up to.

This should have been the moment to just forget it, to give up and go home, and had I known exactly where I was perhaps this is what I might have done. But with persistence I found the house and more importantly the garden, for it was in the garden that I made an important discovery. It was this: I knew nothing.

I have a photograph from that day, taken by Nick (the sculptor) of his six students at work. In the corner of the gazebo I am a grainy shadow, looking down at my stone. Just outside, in the daylight, a woman in a blue jumper is hunched over her bench, concentrating intently on her work. A man with grey hair is holding a drill. There are trees all around us. I don't remember names or faces, though I do remember the tent occasionally shaking with the breeze that picked up as the afternoon wore on, and in the photo there are ripples in canvas confirming exactly this.

Only the previous year I'd completed a doctorate on medieval sculpture and because of this could legitimately call myself Dr Alex Woodcock. But what did I really know? In that moment, standing in a Somerset garden, the answer was *not very much*.

It didn't seem like it at the time, but this was, in fact, excellent news. I had much more to learn and in a different, practical way. And while I didn't want to pin too much on it, I'd also hoped that working stone might help lead me out of my post-PhD gloom. When 'the head and the hand are separate', as Richard Sennett puts it in *The Craftsman*, his book that explores the philosophy and value of making something according to a craft tradition, 'it is the head that suffers'. The head had indeed suffered. At the time, I was mentally exhausted, struggling with depression and completely unprepared for life after a project that had occupied my mind continually for three and a half years. Stone suggested something unyielding to me, something I wanted to find in myself. Perhaps the process of making, of using my hands and my head, might rally those parts that weren't burnt out, and allow those that were time to recover.

Nick had asked all of us to bring a photograph of something

to the workshop, an image or a design that we might try to carve into stone. After much deliberation I settled on the font inside All Saints Church in Combeinteignhead, Devon. I'd visited this church, tucked into the undulating and wooded land on the western side of the River Teign, the previous winter. In the afternoon's darkness the abstract designs carved into the bowl were so full of life and movement that they seemed to glow. At the top of the bowl there was a band of stars, and beneath them were eight unevenly spaced roundels carved with geometric and foliate motifs.

With Nick's workshop coming up in Somerset I remembered this font and its lively carved roundels. I hadn't taken a photo of it at the time, so I went to Exeter library where I discovered an article by Kate Clarke in the *Transactions of the Devonshire Association*: published in 1916, it was one of a series she'd written on the Romanesque fonts of Devon, and included a picture of the Combeinteignhead one. I took a photocopy and glued it into my notebook, in readiness for the afternoon's lesson. Three of the roundels were clear but one stood out: a four-petalled rosette surrounded by large raised dots.

Now, my first stonecarving weathers gently in my parents' garden, counterpoint to the plastic meerkats that my Dad keeps in a nearby border. My carving is shallow, uneven, barely scratching the surface. Nick had asked me, at one point in the afternoon, whether I'd carved stone before. Optimistically I took his comment to be a good sign, a teacher surprised by his pupil's work and an indication of a dormant talent, but thinking about it now he may have just been asking a straightforward question. *Have you carved stone before?* No, was my answer. But I'd spent years looking at medieval sculpture. Perhaps those years had simply been preparation for that moment – yes, preparation for work rather than the work itself, a way into beginning to understand something, not the understanding itself.

I'd left the workshop that day with a tentative carving at best, the edges of the small circles rough and transitioning sharply from the sawn face of the block to my chisel marks, the rosette petals thin and feral. It was only a sketch, an indication of what I could do if I applied myself, perhaps of where I might go next; and the more I looked the more I felt that something lived in its lines and shadows, something definitely worth pursuing. In the simplicity and ancientness of the design there was both familiarity and strangeness, a sense of the past connected to the present, the stone mediating between the two. The stone was of the past but connected to the present, both in the simplicity and ancientness of the design. Dozing on the train home, I imagined a future for myself covered in dust in an airy workshop, an unprecedented ease of movement in my limbs as I worked ever more complex pieces. Walking through the dark streets of Exeter from St David's to Central, to pick up a connecting service, I carried that stone carving like a small, sleepy child against my chest.

There is a mystical pull to stone. It is the raw material of the earth, a handshake away from the basic elements themselves. We associate it with longevity, origins. We say something is 'carved in stone' if it is binding and unalterable. We use it to commemorate the dead, cutting the names of the lost into its fabric, connecting them with the long cycles of geology and perhaps, by doing so, immortality. Depending on the type of stone and how it is worked it can be either low status or high status, ballast or palace. In archaeological terms it is the first age. Stone has served us since the very beginnings: tools, building materials, art.

When I entered into this practical dialogue with stone I did so from a specific time and place: twelfth-century Devon (via a library photocopier in Exeter) and those roundels of the Combeinteignhead font. This period of work is known as Romanesque, and it has captivated me ever since. The Romanesque, especially of South West England, is also where I began my life as a stone carver. A few months after the workshop, I applied for a place on a stonemasonry and conservation course at Weymouth College. This led to a qualification, and persistence in looking for work led to a job, at Exeter Cathedral, where I worked for six years. But in 2014 I decided to leave. I was moving to Cornwall.

There were both practical and emotional reasons for this move.

I'd been offered a place on a course at Falmouth University, one that I'd wanted to do for years. I accepted it because I wanted to go somewhere and do something new, and the fantasy of Cornwall – the blinding sand, the subtropical plants, the Atlantic storms – had sunk in deep. I was up for escape, though. The days had become more and more of a struggle as a prolonged break-up with my partner flattened my world and the city felt less and less like home. It, too, was changing as new development occurred, and it seemed that what I was seeing on the outside mirrored what I felt on the inside. As buildings bloomed from behind hoardings everything began to feel more and more unfamiliar and closed-in. Even the moorhens that had lived in an overgrown cut that fed the River Exe and whose tiny, determined lives I'd enjoyed as part of each morning on the riverside stretch of my commute had had their protective overhanging buddleias stripped away in advance of some quayside regeneration. I felt a camaraderie with them. Clearing out seemed like the best option.

Cornwall had become a place of retreat and refuge. My recent discovery was the Paddington-to-Penzance night train, which stopped at Exeter St David's at four on a Saturday morning. Some nights, with the desire for adventure keeping me awake, I'd be up, out and picking my way carefully through the chaos of nights out still in progress, a bag over my shoulder, to get to the station. Nodding westwards with dozing companions, I'd wake up four hours later with a cup of tea on the sea wall. Something about the stern granite buildings and the salt-laden air, or perhaps the horizontal rain, helped shift my thoughts toward the elemental and away from everything unhelpful. Like everyone else, I was just trying to stay dry.

Sorting through my belongings before moving, I rediscovered the notebook that I'd taken to Nick's garden in Somerset. Ten years had passed, but still the stone dust of that afternoon was lodged in the spiral binding. I had a flick through, stopping at the image of the Combeinteignhead font. I wondered why it had held my attention so much back then and made me want to copy it. Was it the overall design, the wayward spacing of the motifs that seemed to float across the surface of the stone? Or was it the inventiveness of the designs themselves? What was it about Romanesque sculpture that really gripped me? Like the raw recruit I was on that first day, carefully copying a roundel from a Devon font into the surface of my stone, I needed to know more.

I had already packed two of my favourite books on Romanesque sculpture, George Zarnecki's pioneering *English Romanesque Sculpture 1066–1140* and *Later English Romanesque Sculpture 1140–1210*, both published in the early 1950s. I dug them out of a nearby box. Leafing through the black-and-white photographs reminded me of the strength of this work: the dreamlike figures, the masks with beaks and staring eyes; animals stretching into new versions of themselves, tails becoming leaves, feathers patterned like scales; humans standing between lions; processions of figures beneath rosette-like stars; monsters rolling their impossible bodies into waves. These mysterious images are sometimes absent in our museums or galleries. On the whole this is architectural sculpture, part of a functioning building and usually adorning a lintel or capital or tympanum in a medieval church. Despite being on our doorstep, in the towns, villages and countryside throughout Britain and thereby, for the most part, accessible, it's all too easy to pass this work by.

As I replaced the books in their box and carefully pushed bubblewrap into the gaps at each end, I began to realise the significance of my move to Falmouth. I would be much closer to a lot of places I hadn't yet visited and away from the ones that had become familiar. It wasn't just an opportunity to explore why I was so drawn to the Romanesque, but also a chance to retrace the path from carving my first stone to becoming a cathedral stonemason. With the boxes piling up around me, I started to think about some field trips. Exploring old churches is a lifelong pursuit because there is always another one to go and see, so I decided to set some limits. Twelve months seemed about right, I thought. A whole year of looking again and looking anew for these spectacular carvings.

Old buildings can wear their losses well. In truth it's often what we like best about them: the arch that has kinked and slumped, the wing that's been lost to fire and is now repurposed as a romantic ruin. If medieval buildings could remain upright and their sculptured images largely readable after all these centuries then there was still much to learn from them. Perhaps by going out and looking again, looking more closely, I might be able to align myself with this energy that had witnessed every cycle of life. An applied process of grieving on my part for my own losses, moderated through Romanesque sculpture. Secretly, I hoped it might work like a spell to lift the sadness. As the year turned and I'd settled into Falmouth; as the days started to lengthen, offering more light; after the midwinter solstice, in January, that's when I would begin.

At some point in the early 2000s, I picked up a book in the Hartley Library in Southampton and immediately felt a kinship. It wasn't like anything else I'd seen on medieval architecture and sculpture. A brief glance suggested a traditional, conservative – almost dull – book on a niche subject, but close up there beat an unconventional heart. Published in 1909, when the author was forty-six, there was no sense of the pursuit of architectural classification, the lingering dream of the Victorian age, nor much of an attempt to explain the sculptural imagery. Its substantial text ran counter to the mood of the previous fifty years that had understood sculptural 'remnants' of the Romanesque period to be rarities in Cornwall. It took the format of a gazetteer, later perfected by Nikolaus Pevsner's *Buildings of England* series that began forty-two years later, in 1951, with the publication of *Cornwall*. While Pevsner's series gradually took off and is still published today in updated editions, this particular book was a one-off and now long out of print. The book was called *Norman Architecture in Cornwall*, and the writer was Edmund Harold Sedding (1863–1921).

Looking at it now it's easy to see what appealed to me. There is a haphazard quality in which the author is often strikingly present, very much alive, and in command of a vivid sentence. About Crantock he wrote:

Starting from Newquay station [Crantock] … is reached by a winding road in the direction of the Gannel Creek, which, if you're fortunate, you may be able to cross by the narrow plank-bridge, a short cut which the tide allows for about five hours daily. Crossing a stretch of sand you reach the opposite side of the estuary, and wend your way along a lovely wooded lane, rejoicing in the music of birds and the murmur of streamlets running down into the sea.

As you ascend, the horizon broadens, and the broken land unfolds itself before you, bounded by the gleaming ocean.

Passages such as this alternate with architectural descriptions of the churches he visited and their Romanesque sculpture. This combination of writing about nature and architecture lent a different quality to his work compared with other books on the subject. He was an architect himself, a practitioner, which meant that he knew his subject inside out, but he wasn't blinded by his knowledge. He recognised buildings working within a landscape rather than existing purely in the abstract space of the architect's mind. In short, he understood their context, perhaps as a result of his work predominantly in Devon and Cornwall, counties in which it is often impossible to ignore 'the broken land' and the 'gleaming ocean'.

Sedding's drawings also intrigued me. Some were quick sketches, others detailed, careful studies. No doubt there were practical reasons for his reliance upon drawing. Photographic equipment was, in the early years of the twentieth century, cumbersome and expensive. There are photographs in his book but they are few and far between. Sedding, though, may have considered drawing to be a more accurate (or simply more appropriate) means to record historic buildings. He had shown considerable promise as a draughtsman in the early years of his career, winning a Royal Academy medal in 1884, when he was twenty-one, the Royal Institute of British Architects first medal for measured drawings in 1885, and in 1887 a Pugin medal for his sketches.

It would be unfair to compare Sedding's book too closely with one published only a few years later by the artist Auguste Rodin, but the latter's *Cathedrals of France* (1914) shares a surprisingly similar outlook. Both authors connect at an emotional level with medieval sculpture and architecture, praising the combination of subject matter, craft skills, style, material, and perhaps most importantly, the effects of time, which serve to bind it with natural forces and lend it a mysterious quality. Rodin's sketches and notes from his wanderings around some of the great French cathedrals reveal his love for what the medieval sculptors achieved and the impact it had on his own practice. He is keen to defend the work from its detractors and abhorred the repairs he sometimes saw, most in the new wonder material, cement. He wrote of himself as 'a *bridge* connecting two banks, the past to the present', something that Sedding would have immediately grasped.

Sedding's work suggested an instinctive understanding of the Romanesque. In my own pursuit of the Romanesque it seemed obvious where I should start. Of the many churches Sedding restored, there was one he particularly loved: Crantock, on the north coast of Cornwall, where he chose to be buried.

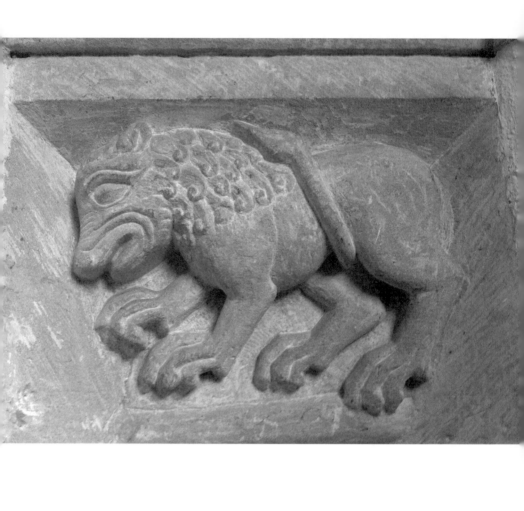

Rediscovering the Romanesque

White birds against blue, gulls afloat on a cliff-edge thermal, motionless beneath the late January sun. Just like them, I wanted to lift off and take flight too, to feel the air solidify around me. It's something I've often felt in high places, a burst of terror or dizziness that dissolves back into the blood as quickly as it pulses through it. An echo of something other, a language unknown or forgotten that presses against the skull with the increase in altitude. Don't look down, some people say, to calm the nerves when up high, but isn't looking up even scarier?

On the cliffs the air was so cold that every breath hurt. Blunted trees clung to a veil of turf; far below, the waves were small, dabs of white froth circling lonely dark rocks. The non-human scale along this stretch of coast has always appealed to me. Even the Atlantic Highway, along which we'd just come, felt like a neglected back road in places, a rat tunnel through copses and along hedgerows. Walking back to the car to continue our journey, I felt the dull echo of an instinct to hunker down out of the wind and rely on whatever remnants of older senses I might muster, like any other creature among the fields and folded slates and glimpses of sea and coves of bright-white sand.

I'd met Marcus on Gyllyngvase Beach on my second night in Falmouth. I'd found a small flat to rent near the seafront, and with everything unloaded the previous day I was sick of unpacking and had gone for a walk by the sea. The only other person on the beach that evening was a man with a metal detector who had stopped to dig something out of the sand. I walked over to say hello and before long we were deep in conversation about all manner of shared interests. We continued the conversation over a pint, where Marcus introduced me to Corella, his partner. It seemed like an auspicious beginning, new friends in a new life, and it wasn't long before we'd hatched plans for a collective field trip. Now here we were, on our way to Crantock.

Usually finding a church is a straightforward task, particularly one I've been to before. But this one seemed to keep moving. We'd left the Atlantic Highway some miles back, and as we got closer I kept seeing the tower appear and disappear behind houses, trees and sudden shifts of gradient. As we drove through Crantock, gardens filled with wind-burnt palms and blue agapanthus filled the windscreen. We stopped at a sandy car park by a grey sea and Marcus turned the car around for another crawl along a narrow lane until an unmistakable piece of masonry, a section of church tower, appeared above the treeline.

St Carantoc was born in 470 AD, the son of a king. Dissatisfied with this accident of birth and perhaps wishing to escape the fate of becoming a king himself, he became a preacher, leaving his native Wales for Ireland, then Cornwall. There is confusion regarding his wanderings, with identical legends about him set in different places, but the mythology is appealing: Crantock church was built where a dove, carrying kindling from his fire, had stopped to rest; a divine sign he had interpreted as favourable.

On a previous visit some months earlier, I'd assumed that the black slate plaque beneath the window in the north transept, almost unreadable in the gloom of the interior, was Sedding's only memorial. 'Remember EDMUND HAROLD SEDDING F.R.I.B.A 1863–1921', it revealed to the light of a torch, 'Architect for the Restoration of this House of God which he greatly loved, 1899–1904'. There was a border of leaves and buds delicately cut into the edges of the slab, surrounding Latin text that paraphrased the last three lines of the Nicene Creed as: 'I acknowledge one baptism for the remission of sins /And I await the resurrection of the dead /And the life of the world to come.' Some weeks later, however, during a lecture at a conference, a photograph flashed before my eyes: Sedding's gravestone. Having searched the churchyard in what I thought was a methodical manner, pacing across the uneven ground between each row of stones (and whispering my apologies to the dead), I didn't know how it could've escaped me. Yet it had. This time, however, I was determined to find it.

The graveyard sloped gently from east to west, with rows of stones arranged in parallel with the path that led from the lychgate to the church. Many of the inscriptions on the graves were hard to read due to the light, a shadow-diffusing mix of pale grey cloud cover and a trace of sea mist. Of necessity my pace slowed, and as I stopped to read each inscription it was easy to see why Sedding chose to be buried here. The air was soft with a tang of earth and salt. Birdsong drowned out a distant engine. Only the angled hedgerows stood as a reminder of winter gales.

Sedding's professional involvement with Crantock began in 1899. By this point he was a well-established architect and had made his name through a number of sensitive restorations of churches, winning awards for his work at Chacewater in Cornwall and St Mary in Newton Abbot. Where possible, Sedding wanted to preserve as much of the original medieval work as he could, resisting the impulse of the Victorian era to revise and in some cases, completely rebuild.

Where did it come from, this receptiveness to the medieval past and its architecture? His early years are marked by tragedy and loss. His father (also called Edmund) died of tuberculosis in 1868, at the age of thirty-two, when Edmund junior was only five. There followed a period when his family struggled to cope, reflected in the dispersal of Edmund and his siblings to relatives and friends. His sister Jessie was sent to an Anglican boarding school in East Grinstead (run by the Sisters of St Margaret, two of whom were her aunts); his brother George went to live with his grandparents in Summertown, Oxford. Edmund himself, aged seven, is noted in the 1871 census as living in a household in Bournemouth.*

Architecture, though, was in his blood. Edmund's father and his uncle, John Dando Sedding, both trained as architects under G. E. Street, a leading practitioner of the Victorian Gothic revival. Edmund senior completed his training first and left to establish his practice in Bristol, then London, and finally Penzance, where he moved on account of his ill health. His brother John joined the practice in 1863, gradually emerging from his elder brother's shadow as a talented and sympathetic restorer of ancient churches. He valued craft skills, learning stonemasonry and metalwork for himself, and was therefore able to understand the materials as well as earn the respect of those craftspeople who worked for him. He also engaged the services of some of the finest artists and decorators of the period, including Edward Burne-Jones and William Morris. Despite these talents and connections, for the Seddings to make their name it would take a combination of chance, wealthy patronage and (for Edmund junior) the discovery of three talented young women.

I'd walked around the churchyard again and again in my mission to find Sedding's gravestone and, frustrated by my inability to do so had given up for the time being, joining Marcus and Corella inside the church. The font caught my eye almost instantly, a minimal twelfth-century work with heads on each corner and a date or an inscription, in illegible numerals and letters, written on one side. There was a border of zigzags around the top of the bowl that were neat in places and off in others. Its four supporting shafts pinned it to the air with precision, the faces at the top of each staring into endless seas of time.

The term 'Romanesque' was first applied to early medieval art and architecture at the start of the nineteenth century. Like

---

* Much of the detail in this chapter about Edmund's life is drawn from the pioneering work of Dr Helen Wilson, particularly her 2016 article 'The Architect Edmund H. Sedding and his Devon Churches', *Transactions of the Devonshire Association*, 255–292.

other descriptive words for art movements and architectural styles (Gothic, for example), it initially harboured negative connotations. Implicit is the sense that it is derivative, a debased form of Roman building traditions. Yet from the start the curiousness of this art suggested a non-Roman pedigree. At first the definition was applied to the broad span of centuries from the end of the Roman Empire to the first stirrings of the Gothic style, approximately 400–1200 AD, but was gradually narrowed to 1000–1200 AD. This marked out its difference from earlier traditions (Byzantine, Carolingian, Saxon) and firmly connected it to, on the Continent, the revival of monasticism and, in Britain, the arrival of the Normans after 1066. The sudden increase of building in stone in this period was part of the wider upturn in artistic and cultural life sometimes known as the Twelfth-Century Renaissance.

Romanesque architecture is defined by several things: round arches, solid masonry walls, small windows, bulky columns. It is an architecture of mass and darkness, quite unlike the subsequent Gothic style, whose characteristic pointed arches directed weight more efficiently, allowing larger windows, and, as a result, more light-filled interiors. Romanesque sculpture is primarily architectural sculpture, meaning it is carved on architectural components of buildings. Ornament is generally focused around doorways and windows. And what ornament it is. Detractors note the 'primitive' tenor of the images, characterised by bold geometric patterns, fantastical creatures and humans in states of rapture or distress, the same chord to which enthusiasts are drawn.

Sedding, of course, was an enthusiast, and in the early 1900s was ahead of the curve. It would take a few more years for the Romanesque to finally emerge from the shadow of the Gothic and be appreciated as a legitimate style. A number of artists led the way in its rehabilitation. Henry Moore, for example, was drawn to the monumentality of the carvings in the church at Adel in Yorkshire, while John Piper's prints and paintings of churches often emphasised geometric Romanesque decoration. The French artist Fernand Léger wrote that in Romanesque sculpture he had found a starting point for his experiments with distortion. Abstract, figurative and decorative at once, Romanesque sculpture appeared to combine freely many of the elements in which twentieth-century artists were interested, and the increasing acceptance of their work gradually liberated what was deemed acceptable study. As the art historian Meyer Schapiro wrote in 1961, the 'values of modern art have led to a more sympathetic and objective approach to exotic arts than was possible fifty or a hundred years ago'. For the Romanesque, modern art was critical in widening its appeal.

The Gothic revival had begun much earlier and by the middle of the nineteenth century was almost the preferred national style, carried out by practitioners like G. E. Street. If this had been driven by aesthetics and mood, as it was during the eighteenth century at Horace Walpole's Strawberry Hill House in Twickenham, it soon turned to scientific study and craft. The Gothic Revival needed craftsmen and women as much as it did architects and academics, and within this, the Arts and Crafts movement – a shift towards the handmade in the face of increasing industrialisation – provided encouragement and focus for artists, designers and architects.

This is where three sisters, Mary, Ethel and Violet Pinwill from Ermington in Devon, enter the picture. In 1873 Henry Bingham Mildmay, a financier at Barings Bank, bought Mothecombe House in the South Hams and properties around Holbeton, east of Plymouth, and started a programme of improvements to buildings which included the churches at Holbeton and Ermington. It was when the restoration work began at Ermington that the Pinwill sisters were taught to carve. Their mother, Elizabeth Pinwill, had asked the chief woodcarver on the project to give all her seven daughters tuition, and three of them excelled. Mary, Ethel and Violet set up their own workshop in a room above the stables at the vicarage and by 1889, before the restoration work at Ermington was complete, were already taking other commissions for substantial pieces of work. They went into business together as Rashleigh, Pinwill & Co and are listed in the 1891 census (aged just twenty, eighteen and seventeen) as professional woodcarvers.* Long before women were even allowed to vote, the Pinwills were running a successful business and producing innovative, beautiful wood carvings for restoration projects throughout the South West.

Mildmay's wealth meant that the architect appointed for the works at Holbeton, John Dando Sedding, had a rare opportunity: to show what could be done to restore an ancient building if money were no object. The work at Ermington church had much less money earmarked for it, and was handed to his nephew Edmund. This decision would turn out to have a profound impact upon not only that particular project, but many others in the South West of England, as Edmund became a close friend of the Pinwill family and used his growing reputation as an architect to bring commissions their way.

In 1891, Edmund relocated from London to Plymouth, setting up his architectural practice next to the Pinwills' workshop and thereby replicating his uncle's relationship with Morris & Co. This was an enduring bond. When Edmund moved his business to Athenaeum Street in London, in 1896, Rashleigh, Pinwill & Co. moved too.

If the work at Crantock was a triumph for Edmund, it was also a high point of the Pinwills' woodcarving. The bench tops, which he designed, have strong Art Nouveau influences. On one, a dove hides within a frame of drooping leaves and slender buds; on another, a poppy in a field appears to be caught in a light breeze; on the ends of a bench itself, fish linger among drifting weeds. The carvings seem entirely appropriate to their setting, as if the door to the church had been left open, allowing some seeds to blow in and sprout into rich foliage, enough to house one or two curious birds.

Back outside in the churchyard I was determined to find Edmund's place of rest. But the light was still muted and without strong contrast it was hard to read many of the inscriptions in the stones, cut, as most were, into granite, an ideal home for lichens which further obscured the words. I sat down at the top of the yard, next to a hedgerow. The ground was woven with moss and damp, so

---

* Edmund Harold Sedding, aged 27, is also listed as a visitor to the Pinwill residence on the day of the census return. Violet died in Plymouth in 1957, aged 83.

I arranged my bag beneath me and sat on that.

There is a particular atmosphere to a graveyard that often concentrates the mind, lending an acute sensitivity to beginnings and endings. My failure to find Edmund Sedding's stone had thrown me, and thinking about his past and how he ended up here had got me thinking about my own. How and why had I found the Romanesque?

In some parts of the South West the past hangs like a veil across the land, refusing to fully make way for the present. As an animal might look up while calmly nibbling a leaf, registering some presence to which we are otherwise oblivious, the invisible mist of days lived long ago might similarly trip some long-dormant biological switch in us. I've felt it throughout much of this part of England, but there are places where it feels concentrated. The stretch of coast between Tintagel and Hartland, where the cliffs are folded and bent and weathered is one of them. Another is between Dorchester and Bridport, where the land steadily rises and the fields on either side of the A35 are pockmarked with round barrows, secret woods and the occasional standing stone. It was in Dorset – and particularly around Christchurch, where my aunt lived – that I first became aware of this feeling in my teens.

In the watery landscape where the rivers Stour and Avon meet, before flowing out to sea, is a building with which I became fascinated: Christchurch Priory. In particular, I liked the highly decorated Romanesque north transept – there was something about the repeated geometric lines of the blind arcading and lozenge-shaped mouldings that made it look fantastic, unexpected and out of place. There were other buildings and features nearby that also appealed: fragments of the castle on its motte; the remains of the Constable's House with its Romanesque window; the marble mausolea whose desolate curves were accentuated by sympathetically planted trees. I started to collect postcards of places that I'd yet to visit but that felt similarly otherworldly to me, like St Catherine's Chapel at Abbotsbury in a thick morning mist, or the nearby Long

Bredy barrow at sunset. These places seemed to carry an indefinable energy, as if they were anchored in time, yet outside of it too.

Encouragement in connecting with this unstable sense of the past came in my discovery of Peter Ackroyd's novels *Hawksmoor* (1985) and *First Light* (1989), both of which suggested that time may be an energy, pooling in some areas, free-flowing in others. In *First Light*, which is centred around a long barrow in the Dorset landscape (and therefore primed to my sensibilities), time becomes a psychic whirlwind that draws in the archaeologists investigating the monument, the farmers who have worked the land for centuries, and the long-dead builders of the barrow. *Hawksmoor* explored the darkness of buildings and foundation sacrifices, occult geometries, languages no longer spoken. The energy of these books seemed to come from a sense of incompletion, in which the past was malleable. As Timothy Walsh puts it referencing Rodin's obsession with fragments: incomplete works 'have a greater power on the imagination'. I'd discovered a secret: the humble and broken artefact, ruined building or piece of weathered masonry allow us to time travel.

Real and imaginary versions of the past were also colliding in the music I was listening to around then. I'd given up early-eighties pop for mid-eighties metal, which had ended up at late-eighties Sisters of Mercy. The conspicuous presence of pasts, real or not, in the artwork and lyrics of bands such as the Sisters, Fields of the Nephilim, Bauhaus and others piqued my interest in the medieval ruins that could be found throughout East Sussex where I grew up: Pevensey, Bayham Abbey and Battle. Some of my music discoveries had come from the friends I'd made through skateboarding, which had encouraged me to seek out parts of my town that were abandoned, semi-ruinous or simply closed. Where the plants were moving in was generally where the people were moving out, and this often meant a new skate spot was available: factories, car parks, industrial units. We were street skaters and unwelcome in most places, but the edges were ours. In a way, the music and skateboarding of my teens had attuned me to the ruinous, and to how nature, left alone for long enough, could reclaim human spaces.

Later, my studies in archaeology would draw many of these themes together. I was lucky enough to get funding for a degree and then again for postgraduate research. In York I spent one summer recording the interior of a medieval church: All Saints in North Street, famous for its stained glass. I spent a lot of time drawing the columns to record the stone indents that might reveal the position of former screens and by inference, lost medieval chapels. During these quiet weeks I began to notice the architectural sculpture more and more. Despite the modern lighting and the summery light outside it was often in shadow, partially hidden in the vaulting of the roof or some other crepuscular location. This was a characteristic not lost on some of the earlier writers on the subject. The French art historian Émile Mâle (1862–1954) wondered how likely it was that the carvers 'would have attempted to express so many and such subtle meanings through figures which are invisible from below except with good glasses?'

Mâle's point was a good one. It would take me years of study to explore what these images might have meant to their makers and viewers, only to discover that there were no straightforward or easy answers. During this time, and in the reverse of the artists who each found something sustaining within the Romanesque for their practice, I discovered a latent artistic talent through it. With my photographs usually blurred by distance and technical inability, I would try to draw the images instead, sometimes from the picture but more often than not directly at the site, as Edmund Sedding had done. I didn't realise it immediately, but contact with the stone carvings was beginning to produce a creative response in me. I started to experiment with oils, linocuts and other prints of the imagery as well. The house I shared in Southampton began to fill up with geometric motifs and mythical creatures in assorted media. I'd opened a door and medieval sculpture had crept in. From here, it wasn't really too much of a leap to begin to think about trying to carve stone itself.

★

I heard a shout from the other side of the churchyard, breaking my train of thought. I'd not noticed Corella come out of the church but there she was, parting clumps of grass around the base of a large granite memorial: Sedding's gravestone. A circle-headed cross set upon a square granite plinth – nothing like the image in my mind.

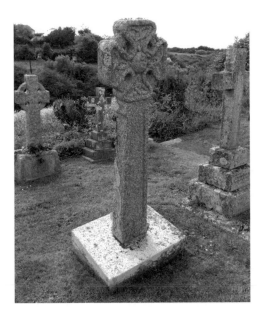

It leaned forward at such an angle that his name was hidden in the long grass, a simple inscription cut in shallow letters. Like his plaque in the north transept, it was nearly impossible to read. I had to feel for the shape of the letters, to trace their outlines with my fingertip. Similar to the medieval stone sculptors whose work still carried traces of their life, Sedding's presence was also an absence.

Leaving Crantock, I wondered where to go next. I'd begun to get a strong sense of Sedding's religious motivations: as part of the work he undertook at Shaldon in south Devon, for example, he had installed a stone altar. This was a clear sign of where his sympathies lay, as altars made of stone had been illegal since the Reformation, and he was forced to remove it by the church authorities. Yet for someone so attuned to the medieval past he wrote little about the images he found carved among the twelfth-century churches, deferring instead to architectural detail and measurements, skimming over some of the more interesting features. I was wondering just how much context he could give me. I wanted to find out more about the images that had helped to launch my practice.

Leafing through a copy of the updated edition of Pevsner's *Cornwall* later that evening back in Falmouth, I stopped on an unusual photo: a tympanum carved with what appeared to be two large cats sheltering beneath the languid arms of a palm tree, the tails of each beast curled upwards to waft the air by their ears. It was at the church of St Gregory, Treneglos, in east Cornwall. Something about this pairing of exotic creatures – perhaps lions – and rural location intrigued me. It seemed an ideal place to start to look a little closer at the images themselves.

The Treneglos Lions

The silence at St Gregory's was overpowering. It rose up from the wet earth and mosses on the granite post to meet my hand on the metal gate. My waterproof coat was suddenly very loud, as were my feet on the ground. Standing still, I could hear my heart beating and didn't want to move or even breathe, so seductive was this quiet. The church stood in a circular enclosure ringed with trees, branches like charcoal lines against the sky. Above, crows watched my slow progress to the porch. Slate gravestones wore anemone-like lichens. I could see the dark semicircular shape of the carved tympanum above the south door, a smudge in the shadows of the porch. As I stepped closer, the outlines of the two creatures emerged.

Artists, writes Rebecca Solnit, through presenting perplexing situations or by asking unanswerable questions, 'push us into the dark'. Their work confronts us with the unknown or mysterious aspects of life to which there are only more questions and no particularly satisfying answers. Solnit's phrase kept repeating in my mind as I stood in the churchyard of St Gregory. As my eyes adjusted to the sickly grey light that hung beneath the roof of the porch, partially concealing the tympanum, I could see that her statement, written in the twenty-first century, was just as applicable to the twelfth. Like a tide coming in and then retreating, the Romanesque had left behind its own strand line of imagery that now appeared as fragments of things from another world. It seemed as alien as a fallen meteorite in this silent village, and in the quiet I contemplated the other unknowns that it opened up, the new darknesses that it might trail behind it.

The creatures resembled chunky-looking cats but, as Sedding wrote, were 'probably meant for lions'. They faced each other on either side of a tree trunk, their pointed ears and tails angled upwards below the tree's volcano-shaped leaves and wandering branches. Though it was carved in high relief, in the half-light of the porch, the image appeared to shrink back into the stone, 'a kind of local green slate' known as Ventergan, which was already recorded in the early twentieth century as flaking badly.*

Carvings like this bring to mind some words by the sculptor Mark Batten, a contemporary of Henry Moore and Eric Gill. In his book *Stone Sculpture by Direct Carving*, published in 1957, he captioned the photograph of an eleventh-century capital from Canterbury Cathedral in Kent with a cheery, 'easily within the powers of a beginner or amateur'. I've always loved this encouraging quote, even if it isn't true, no matter how disarmingly basic Romanesque sculpture can sometimes appear.

Batten's book was a real discovery. I'd found it in a book sale at Southampton City Library towards the end of my PhD research. I didn't know about it, which perplexed me. I'd spent years researching medieval sculpture, which meant I was aware of most books on the subject, but opening *Stone Sculpture* it became clear why: it wasn't a book about art history or criticism, it was a book about *doing*. It had a different tone to my usual reading. It wasn't impartial but impassioned and insistent. Batten spoke directly, making the case that you – or I – could do this, though warned that there were no short cuts to practice. He urged students to go and look at Romanesque buildings, for they represented a 'Golden Age of masonry and sculpture'. It was possible, it was all possible, if you got yourself a few tools and just got on with it. There was a photo of him working away, carving a head *in situ* on a label stop to a church window. I admired his confidence and skill. Could I leap the chasm

---

* The stone takes its name from the farm at Fentrigan in Warbstow parish near where it was quarried.

from theory to practice? I didn't know if I could.

Batten wrote about the 'exquisite proportion and feeling in the design' of Romanesque sculpture. He would have liked Treneglos. If at first glance the carving appeared simple, certain features gradually revealed a greater complexity. The carver had used the design to fill the space of the tympanum, keeping the work of removing stone to a minimum. The result was a healthy balance between empty space and image, presence and absence, which allowed strong shadows and a clear reading of the work. I'd a sense that the carver who made this piece was well used to fitting the unusual creatures of the Romanesque bestiary into cramped architectural spaces. There was a sense of delight in the beasts with their sinuous tails that echoed the curves of the tree's long branches.

Sedding too, I was sure, would have something pertinent to say about this carving, which was why I'd brought him with me on my trip. Fishing my copy of *Norman Architecture in Cornwall* out of my bag, I sat down on one of the stone benches that lined each side of the porch. This book had its own history: it was given to me by an archaeologist friend and had been signed at some point in ink on the pale, marbled end-paper, 'D. Eyre', along with a palimpsest of stamped and embossed addresses and library class marks. Chief among these was that of La Retraite, Burnham-on-Sea, Somerset, Telephone 2968 – La Retraite was a convent school for girls, opened in 1888 in the burgeoning seaside resort on the north Somerset coast. I imagined that Sedding, with his Catholic leanings, would have been pleased that his book had made it into the library of a convent.

Sedding had this to say about St Gregory's:

As this fabric was rebuilt in 1858, much of its architectural value has been lost to the county, for mediaeval walls cease to be old when they have once been pulled down; and with the reconstruction all the old benches and screens have gone too. Some remnants of the carved roofs may be seen in the south porch, from which it may be readily assumed that the old roofs were of beautiful character. The Norman tympanum over the south doorway has been saved, and may be seen in the wall immediately above the square-headed sixteenth-century doorway; and moreover, it probably stands in its ancient position. It is a valuable relic in Cornwall, where so few remain in anything like a good condition. In this example the relief is unusually high, varying from three-quarters to half an inch in depth. It is, however, not a good specimen of Ventergan stone, and large pieces are now ready to shale off.

On the opposite page there was a sketch in pen and wash of the tympanum, cartoon lions and a tree resembling a seaside inflatable palm. I remembered that there was something similar at the nearby church of St Petrock and St Keri in Egloskerry; I flicked through the pages to find that Sedding had drawn this one too, a hazy sketch initialled simply with a capital S and dated 1902. The Egloskerry tympanum is carved with a dragon, its body writhing into a figure of eight and its head turned back to face its waving tail. Technically it was a wyvern, a dragon with two legs instead of four, and no wings. I was struck by the similarities between it and the Treneglos beasts, particularly in the style of the leaves of its tail compared to the foliage of the tree at Treneglos.

Perhaps I was reading too much into these pieces to think that they were created by the same hand, but what I was more certain of was their subject matter. From my research I knew that paired or lone beasts, in particular lions and dragons, were regulars on the tympana and fonts of Romanesque England, especially in combination with a central tree or other foliate motif. In the South West, there are lions with a tree at Milborne Port (Somerset) and a centaur and a lion with a tree at Stoke-sub-Hamdon (also in Somerset). On the fonts at Bodmin and St Newlyn East in Cornwall the central tree is a sprig of foliage and the creatures are lions. At Down St Mary in Devon, the tails of the two lions that appear on either side of a figure sprout into foliage themselves.

Monstrous and exotic creatures might seem odd above a doorway into an English church, but this was imagery with a long pedigree. Like much of the imagery that filtered into Romanesque art, the Tree of Life flanked by animals or birds was originally a Near-Eastern motif and already ancient by the time it was being carved at Treneglos in the twelfth century. The tree fitted well with many crucial

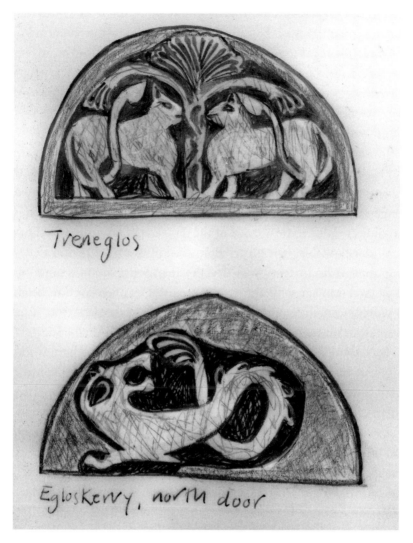

Treneglos

Egloskerry, north door

aspects of Christian mythology, from the awakening to knowledge in the Garden of Eden to immortal life through the crucifixion. Resurrection and renewal, as well as the transience of life, appear to be persistent themes in its imagery throughout Romanesque and Gothic sculpture. The associated animals and mythical beasts were likely to be closely connected to this pool of meanings. Dragons, certainly, were not always symbols of darkness. The wyvern, for example, appears on the shields of Norman soldiers in the Bayeux

Tapestry, which suggested that it might be thought of as a symbol of strength and power. Not until the end of the medieval period did the multiple meanings of the dragon narrow to an almost universal interpretation of the creature as evil. Before then, the carving of these images on a tympanum placed directly above a doorway may have strengthened the idea that salvation and renewal were to be found within the building.

In medieval culture, churches were considered liminal places: thresholds between one space and another, places where the supernatural merged with the everyday. This meant that they were dangerous. As our medieval ancestors understood, users of these buildings needed to be warned of the danger as well as protected from it. Understandably, it is on religious buildings of the period that we find apotropaic imagery well developed. Apotropaic means to 'turn away', so an image with apotropaic qualities was perceived to be able to protect something, in this case a building and its users, from attack by a power ultimately derived from a divine or semi-divine source.

Broadly, apotropaic imagery might be understood to have worked in one of two ways. First, the image could repel malevolent spirits by using concentrated images of abundant life force: impossible monsters (themselves understood to be generated by sexual transgressions), images of violence, exaggerated body parts such as the head or genitalia, and so on. Much of what we describe as grotesque now falls into this category. Then there are the complex and repeated patterns. These, as the anthropologist Alfred Gell has suggested, slow perception down, rendering demons harmless by trapping them in the complexity of the design. Either way, apotropaic images were intended to charm the viewer, human or otherwise, into a kind of paralysis, and by doing so avert any potentially harmful outcomes.

To get a closer look at the Treneglos lions I stood on the bench. With my eyes now level with the lower part of the sculpture I could see the depth of relief more clearly. Flakes of stone were peeling off around the edges and across the bodies of the animals, perhaps a reminder that before the restoration of 1858 that rebuilt the body of the church (and probably its tower), the carving was outside and exposed to the elements. Patrons were aware that sculpture, then as now, took time and skill, and that their investment was also a symbol of wealth and status. Patronage was the reason why this carving existed at all. But who was responsible for it? Why was it here in this part of Cornwall?

As I left the churchyard on that March afternoon, the crows struck up a deafening corvid clatter. I'd been inside the porch long enough for them to forget me; my sudden appearance in the centre of their territory sent shock waves through the trees.

At the bottom of the slope that led up to the platform I heard the train pull out from Falmouth Town station. The next one to Truro wasn't for another half an hour, so instead of waiting around I walked to nearby Gyllyngvase Beach. I made my way over to the exposed rocks and concrete sea defences to a spot where I could sit and look out across the water, which was barely moving on this overcast day. Pendennis Castle and the lighthouse at St Anthony Head marked the start of the Fal estuary over to my left, and to my right a backcombed mass of trees crested the cliffs west of Swanpool. The bay was the colour of steel. Several container ships lay at anchor, one of them an alarmingly bright orange.

It was a few days since my visit to Treneglos and the images were still fresh in my mind, not just the lions but the wyvern at nearby Egloskerry too. I was still wondering about any potential connection between them, so had been pleased to find an article written by Arthur Langdon in the first volume of the *Victoria County History for Cornwall*. Here he'd included a page of line drawings of all the sculptured Romanesque tympana that had survived in the county. He'd arranged the drawings so that it was instantly possible to see that, of the work that had survived, the carvers in Cornwall favoured certain themes. Predominantly these were the Agnus Dei (the 'lamb of God', usually a generic four-legged beast with one foreleg crooked back to support the end of a cross) which could be found at Egloskerry on a second tympanum (inside, above the south door), St Michael Caerhayes, Perranaworthal, St Thomas's in Launceston, and on a voussoir at St Anthony in Roseland. Then there were the geometric designs largely based upon circles such as Rame, Mylor, Launceston and Cury; and finally the creatures at Treneglos and Egloskerry. Langdon's drawings made it even easier to notice that the almond-shaped eyes of the Egloskerry lamb and something about the spacing of the entire carving with its clear lines and overall asymmetry did suggest a connection between it, the wyvern outside, and the Treneglos piece. It was difficult not to conclude that these sculptures were the products of the same workshop, or even the same carver, one who was aware of trends in imagery occurring elsewhere.

The development of sculpture in eleventh- and twelfth-century England followed a different path to that on the Continent. Traditions of crosses, for example, carved with figures and ornament, were quite out of step with the new architectural sculpture evolving on the mainland. Sculpture was largely independent of architecture. As the scholar George Zarnecki puts it, 'Anglo-Saxon reliefs were pinned to the wall as flowers or jewels would be to a dress, without being an integral part of it.' The spread of the Romanesque style in the wake of the Norman Conquest changed all this, and sculpture and architecture became intertwined. Carved capitals were crucial in this development, initially starting as simplified versions of the Roman Corinthian order, with volutes and flute-like foliage and sometimes incorporating geometric or figurative motifs. Increasingly, however, other architectural details were also carved: doorways, tympana, lintels and arches. By the beginning of the twelfth century there was a 'general blossoming of sculpture' that spread to all parts of Continental Europe. This included the South West of England, where, in common with the rest of the British Isles, church building took off, as evidenced by the Norman masonry widely traceable in churches throughout the region.

Behind where I was standing on the seafront, sections of the concrete wall had been used for graffiti. I got up and stretched my legs. It was odd to see graffiti here, right next to the sea – it seemed out of place. There were slogans, entertaining observations, even portraits. Bright pink and yellow clashed with the green of the shrubs and other nearby creepers hanging over the edge of the low cliff. It was high quality, but then Falmouth is a town full of art students. The jolts of the spray paint reminded me that, in addition to Mark Batten's encouraging book, it was art students who finally gave me the shove I needed to go and learn stone carving for myself.

It was a few months after I'd made my first piece in Somerset, and was accidental again, like everything of value seems to be. I'd got a job as a library assistant at the University of Plymouth, but as I got to know and work with the students I began to realise that I was on the wrong side of the desk: I wanted to make something too. I remember the palpable sense of excitement at one of the degree shows and the wide variety of work, from handcrafted furniture to adventurous installation pieces, which included one awkward-looking construction made from MDF, about the size of a small room. Inside it was like a maze, and through a labyrinth of successively darker, smaller, and, so it seemed, quieter, spaces, it focused the attention on one or two simple images, each sparsely lit. The experience evoked such an unexpected sense of wonder and awe that I found myself moved, and I left the show with a profound feeling that I had more to offer. My afternoon carving stone had gone deeper than I'd thought.

A delayed train meant I arrived in Truro much later than I'd hoped. As I apologised to the staff on the desk at the Royal Cornwall Museum and headed up the stairs to the Courtney Library, I tried to remember the list of books that I'd asked the librarian to get out for me: a copy of Sedding's *Norman Architecture in Cornwall* (so that I didn't have to bring my own), a back issue of *Cornish Archaeology* (to check a reference in an article I'd either forgotten to make a note of or misplaced), and a copy of the updated edition of the Pevsner *Buildings of England* guide for the county (because it is always useful to have at hand). I'd also asked for anything relating to the medieval architecture and sculpture of the county, so I was looking forward to seeing what else had been selected for me.

The rain was hammering on the windows so I was glad to be at my destination at last and thankful for the warmth. Hanging my coat by the door, I signed in and was directed to a space at the long table that ran along the centre of the room. A stack of books waited for me. As well as the ones I'd requested there was *Cornwall and the Cross* by Nicholas Orme, a fantastically readable account of medieval Christianity in the county; the longer and more detailed second volume of the *Victoria County History for Cornwall*, from which it drew, and the *Early Cornish Sculpture* volume of the Corpus of Anglo-Saxon Stone Sculpture.

The churches of Treneglos and Egloskerry were only a few miles from Launceston so I decided to begin there, to see what was going on in the eleventh and twelfth centuries, and very quickly discovered its importance to the county. In the late eleventh century, Launceston was the chief town in Cornwall, and its development owed as much to its geography – a strategic position near a fordable stretch of the River Tamar – as it did to one man: Robert, Count of Mortain (*c.*1031–1090). Robert was the half-brother of William the Conqueror. His prominent role in the invasion of England is remembered in his depiction in the Bayeux Tapestry, where he is shown advising William and his half-brother, Odo, after the landing at Pevensey. After the Conquest, as reward for his support, William gave him a large amount of property, and by 1086, with almost eight hundred manors from Sussex to Yorkshire to Cornwall, as well as valuable castles such as Pevensey, Robert was the greatest landholder after the King and the Church.

Robert was also given the task of governing Cornwall, and established Launceston as the centre of his power. It prospered under his influence and the remains of his castle still loom over the town. It was customary for a Norman lord to have a religious house nearby whose clergy would pray for him and his family, and many brought small communities of French monks over to England with them. Robert did not do this, however. Instead he turned to the established minster of St Stephen.

It is difficult to reconstruct this period with great clarity, but in many respects Robert was no different to other ruling figures before him, enriching himself and rewarding his followers using the estates and land belonging to the church to do so. It is almost certainly the case that the decline in value of much of the land and property owned by the churches of the county in this period can be attributed to him. Yet in his support for the minster of St Stephen there is a glimmer of compassion, and as a result it would become the main church in Cornwall to benefit from the Norman Conquest, entering into a relationship with the lords of Launceston Castle that continued through much of the twelfth century. Indeed, this connection would make it the best-endowed and wealthiest religious house in the county for much of the medieval period.

Against this background of wealth and high-status patronage it's fitting that here, at the church that remains from this priory, we find the only examples of Romanesque figure sculpture in the county. These take the form of two panels, discovered during renovation work in 1883 and now set into the wall at the east end of the chancel. Both are carved in a volcanic stone and depict recognisable Christian motifs: one, a seated figure of Christ in Majesty; the other, the Virgin and Child. Both stones are damaged, not only from being reused as building material in the post-medieval period, but possibly from deliberate iconoclasm prior to being walled up (the head of the infant Christ, for example, is missing). Nonetheless, these are important pieces of sculpture in the South West – the nearest similar examples being in Somerset at Congresbury and Langridge. There is debate over their date, but the late eleventh or early twelfth century is probable. They indicate that Launceston, which was already a thriving commercial and administrative centre in the Anglo-Saxon period, had become the capital of Cornwall by the beginning of the twelfth century, under the guiding hand of the counts of Mortain.

The Mortains' power ended in 1106 when Count William, who succeeded his father Robert in 1090, quarrelled with Henry I and lost his English lands and titles. The start of the twelfth century also marked a shift towards the Bishops of Exeter becoming the active rulers of Cornwall. Osbern, who had been Bishop since 1072, died in 1103 and was replaced four years later by William Warelwast, an ambitious and well-connected man close to the king. In 1127, Warelwast converted St Stephen into an Augustinian priory (he had done the same at Bodmin in 1123–24; a successor, Bishop Bartholomew, would do likewise at St Germans in the 1180s). The canons of this order followed different rules to those of their predecessors, living a communal life without personal property and rarely, if ever, leaving the grounds.

New buildings would have been built to suit these regulations, but building work was probably under way before this, perhaps as early as the late eleventh century, under the patronage of Robert himself. Remnants of the church from this date indicate a substantial building with an elaborate east end, in keeping with its status as a collegiate church endowed by the most powerful baron in Cornwall. With control of Launceston, along with four other major churches (Bodmin, Perranzubuloe, Probus and St Kew), William Warelwast used the income to endow the beginnings of his cathedral in Exeter and support the founding of Plympton Priory in Devon. Throughout the twelfth and thirteenth centuries the bishops of Exeter became the most important landowners in Cornwall.

Having read enough to get a sense of the power and importance of Launceston in the 1100s, I started to think that the sculpted tympana at Treneglos and Egloskerry were not unusual, isolated relics. More likely, they were linked to patrons keen to display their status and connections to the nearby power base at Launceston. Along with other fragments of work that remained in the town itself, such as the doorway to the White Hart pub (originally from the priory) carved with ornate lozenge patterns and foliate capitals, and the tympanum reused as walling material at St Thomas's church, cut with giant rosettes and a tiny Agnus Dei, it suggested that sculpture was integral to life in the period – and perhaps part of a wider programme of artistic endeavour around the county.

Another church sometimes mentioned in connection with both

Treneglos and Egloskerry is Tremaine. It too has a tympanum, with tantalising suggestions that it was once carved with a dragon, and later that afternoon I read Sedding's writings on Tremaine. He was in his element here. 'To one whose mind is still full of the memories of some great English Abbey or Cathedral,' he wrote, 'this desolate little sanctuary would seem hardly worthy of notice' but to 'the few who love the work of the medieval craftsmen, these works they have left us are beyond price.' If Sedding was inclined towards a misty-eyed reverie sometimes, his understanding of and feel for these buildings could never be doubted.

I love a small, forgotten church myself, and was easily persuaded by Sedding's enthusiasm: it was time for another field trip, and when I left the library later that day I texted Marcus to see if he was up for joining me. He was, so we set off the following morning, driving the sixty miles north-east from Falmouth to St Winwalo, in the village of Tremaine.

All the signs were good. The road was narrow and, fortunately, empty – there were no passing places. Tall hedgerows offered only occasional glimpses of the landscape beyond, and for the moment, the rain was holding off. The tiny church sat on top of a hill in the centre of a crown of beech trees, its weather-beaten masonry changing colour with the passing clouds whose shadows collected in the fields and woodlands far below. In the distance I thought I could see the sea.

It wasn't difficult to imagine Sedding being taken with this church and its location: standing there on a late-March afternoon with the light folding itself into the rolling hills and the crows swooping through the air, I was too. In the porch there were a few notices including the electoral roll for the parish. There were six parishioners in total. Inside, a plain Romanesque font stood wrapped in a velvet silence. My quest to find the tympanum was momentarily forgotten.

Sedding had sketched the tympanum at St Winwalo, a sorry-looking blank segment containing a circle and a dot, the former the repaired hole where a flue pipe for the boiler was cut through, the small dot perhaps the last bit of sculpted surface. As Arthur Langdon noted, this indent may well have been part of the dragon's tail. Sitting on a pew for a moment I was in no rush to confirm this, enjoying the complete absence of sound and the smell of damp plaster that permeated the nave. In this quietness I found myself thinking about an early essay by Ralph Waldo Emerson, in which he'd said that a sculpture is beautiful only when it ceases to be comprehensible, the stone transitioning from 'that which is representable to the senses to that which is not'. Sculpture as a point of connection with the unseen, the doorway into another world. In the small nave of the church at Tremaine, I could understand that.

A Line in the Cliff

Cornish stone was starting to perplex me. Ever since my first afternoon's stone carving in Somerset, I'd been hoovering up scraps of information here and there about workable stones. Stonemasons, naturally, are concerned with what might go wrong. There's no point putting time and energy into something only to find it falls to pieces halfway through, and for these reasons some stones and particular beds of stones are held in high esteem. Nobody in their right mind would choose to work a piece of Heavitree stone beyond a rudimentary block form, for example, because it's composed of loosely cemented grits and chunks of other stones and crumbles easily. As a building stone, however, it was used from the late medieval to the early modern periods and is responsible for some of Exeter's distinctive red buildings, though most of these have been slowly crumbling away ever since they were put up.

The good stones, the stones that are soft enough to carve but strong enough to withstand the weather: these are the ones. This is why, for the most part, it quickly comes back to a few old faithfuls that have been used for centuries. For much of the South West these are Portland, Ham, Beer and Bath, stones that are consistent, more or less predictable, and, for the most part, still commercially available. In Cornwall the stones favoured by the Romanesque masons tended to be the more unusual ones of the county and this meant, if I were to find out more about them, getting out there to explore the landscapes where the stone was extracted. I wanted to know about the different types of stone available to the medieval masons, how they differed from each other, what they might be like to work. What was an elvan? It was a term I kept coming across in books and articles, but what did it look like? What might it be like to work? I needed not so much a geology refresher as a geology beginner and one specific to the South West, so on a bright day in early April, I set out along the south coast of Cornwall to find the source of one of these stones, a golden-coloured, fine-grained volcanic named after the village where it was quarried: Pentewan.

A few things had prompted this excursion. First, in the Courtney Library a couple of weeks earlier, I'd read that it outcropped in the cliffs nearby, at a place called Polrudden Cove. There was a picture of a strike of gold against grey, an uneven brush of colour in the rock above the waves. This hadn't really meant anything to me at the time, but a few days later I'd visited the church at Lanreath. I was keen to see the Romanesque font, one of a small group in the county with palmette decorations like those at Fowey, Lanlivery and Ladock. I was unprepared, however, for such an incredible piece of work, easily one of the best pieces of freestanding medieval sculpture in Cornwall. This, it turned out, was carved from Pentewan stone.

Then there was my chance find. Walking back from the station one afternoon I'd found a bit of Pentewan – or at least what I thought was a bit of it – in a skip. There was a heap of garden refuse and several other stones, including slates and some rough blocks of granite. Perhaps an old wall had been taken down, as there was plenty of mortar debris in there too. Among all this, a roughly triangular-shaped golden stone caught my eye. I picked it out and took it back to my flat, propping it by the door. Pentewan stone had suddenly appeared in my world and I wanted to find out more about it.

Up on the coast path the air was cold and smelt strongly of seaweed. As I climbed out of the village, I stopped for a moment to peer through a straggle of trees. I could see the St Austell river forming a wide loop across the beach before it emptied into the mirror-like sea. It felt great to be up so high. I carried on walking, and as the path levelled out I was at the edges of fields, right on top of the cliff, with seabirds soaring far below me.

As I walked I thought about the Lanreath font, which had

been critical in showing me the possibilities of this golden stone. Apart from the decoration – an engaging design featuring repeated palmettes – a cable twist and varieties of chevron, the font was carved from a single piece of stone. I imagined how arduous the task of making it must have been, from the removal of a stone block out of the ground, to its transportation somewhere to be carved, and then the carving itself. After squaring it up, then producing a cylindrical form, it would've needed hollowing out and cutting into its waisted shape before the decorative carving could begin. There were traces of paint caught in some of the lines too: a red, earthy colour. From start to finish it must have occupied a skilled individual for several weeks. It represented intense work, something often overlooked when we casually wander around old buildings.

I was pleased to have found a bit of Pentewan stone and thought that, when I got the chance, I'd try and make it into something. I have a professional excuse these days for my stone collecting, but as far as I can remember the urge has always been there. I blame the publisher Usborne for this, fanning the flames of what was a latent childhood interest into a full-blown obsession. The *Usborne Book of Rocks and Minerals* combined a straightforward, clear and educational text enlivened by simple illustrations with a kind of catalogue of rocks, each entry with a space to tick it off once you'd found a sample. I still have the book, its yellow cover faded and wrinkled, as if it's been underwater at some point in its history (there is every chance that it has). Here I first learned about the three main rock types – igneous, sedimentary and metamorphic – and the cycles of plate tectonics and weathering that created and sustained them. Igneous were my favourite from the off: they had crystals that grew from molten liquid, both an exotic start and end point to which my young brain naturally cleaved. I collected specimens of amethyst and rose quartz and even a chunk of bright yellow sulphur. None of them came from anywhere near my home in the South East, or even Britain, which made them even more exciting somehow. Only later did I start to find an interest in stones closer to home.

Bexhill in Sussex, where I grew up and lived until I was eighteen, is sedimentary rock territory. I was reminded of this only the other day as I unfolded a geological map of Britain that was tucked into the back of a textbook: it quickly covered my small table in the library, the coloured bands denoting different types of rock were like a marbled endpaper, unfurling around the South East of England before being chopped up into fragments as they headed north and west. Sedimentary rocks, formed at the surface of the earth from the weathering and deposition of other fragments of rocks, or their chemical precipitation out of bodies of water, seemed less appealing than the igneous ones with their sparkly crystals and intense colours. Still, there was potentially something in them that did grab me, and that was fossils.

Once I'd made the connection between the slumped fragments of cliff that rose and fell to the east of Bexhill Beach and the possibility of them containing dinosaurs, my interest started to pick up. Dinosaurs had definitely walked this way: there is a cast of an Iguanodon footprint in Bexhill Museum, taken from a print found near Galley Hill. I started to collect pieces of sandstone from the Wealden Beds, flints that had fallen out of the chalk and had been smoothed by the waves. Years later, at nearby Pett Level on a geology field trip, I found a fossil ammonite, the cast replaced by the metallic mineral pyrite, glistening with colours like a fuel spill on a wet road. Probably because of this beginning surrounded by crumbly sandstones and chalk I longed for 'proper' rocks like limestones or slates, something substantial that created varied landscapes and wouldn't regularly fall into the sea – much as that possibility thrilled me. Where the map gets complicated, dotted with intrusions and fractured by ancient earth movements, is where my eye was (and is still) drawn. Scotland, Ireland, the north, Devon and Cornwall.

Metamorphic rocks interested me the least back then, though of the three groups they are the ones that intrigue me most now. There is an alchemy about them: given the right circumstances, enough heat and/or pressure, even a rock can change. Their very form is a record of transformation. Limestone recrystallises as marble; sandstone as quartzite. This fluctuation in states can produce some incredible stones. Serpentinite found on the Lizard in Cornwall is one of them, a rare stone that can be a pale green or a dramatic black and red depending on where it outcrops. For some stones there is a specific sequence of change. A dull-looking mudstone will gradually harden into a slate and then, if the circumstances are right, phyllite, then schist, then the black-and-white banded and sometimes quite spectacular gneiss. It's as if the natural processes of the earth are primed to make the ordinary into something full of wonder.

The coast path felt a bit white-knuckle in places and I was praying that the cliff immediately below the turf was stable – there seemed to be a lot of air very close to my feet. From this vantage point I could see the curve of the rock face below and there appeared to be an inlet about half a mile further on; perhaps this was where the Pentewan seam outcropped. The sun was behind me so I was hopeful of being able to make out any changes in colour, of where the pale grey slate that made up most of the cliff might give way to a line of pale gold. The sea was a long way down and an intense deep blue, fringed with white water where it encountered the base of the cliffs.

Before setting out I'd read up as much as I could about Pentewan stone. I'd learned that it was an igneous rock and that its pale golden-yellow colour eventually weathered to a light grey. I'd also discovered that it was known as an 'elvan', a word used in Devon and Cornwall for the native varieties of quartz-porphyry. These are igneous rocks rich in feldspar and mica and similar in composition to granites, but typically with much finer crystals. Elvan dykes, cutting through the surrounding country rock of granites and slates, are often able to be traced for many miles, which meant that the Pentewan seam could be worked at various places (at Polgooth, Sticker and Penrice, for instance), each locality with its own distinctive variety. I'd also read that it was a freestone, which goes some way towards explaining its popularity with the medieval carvers. Freestones can be cut and shaped in any direction without splitting, which makes them easier to work and less likely to fail during the processes of carving.

Elvan was a recent discovery and I was pleased to learn that there was more than one variety. At the other end of the colour scale from Pentewan (a 'white' elvan, despite its golden colour) are the blue elvans. Confusingly, blue elvans are in fact greenstones and greenstones are almost black. Their dark colour is due to a low silica content and high quantities of iron and magnesium (ferromagnesian) minerals. Known in the geological literature as dolerites or diabases, one of the best known is Catacleuse (or Cataclews) stone, which outcrops on the north coast at Harlyn Bay, near Padstow.

Like Pentewan, Catacleuse stone was quarried directly from the cliffs. Charcoal-black with a green or blue tinge and able to be polished, when it will take on a glassy, obsidian-like finish, it was highly suited to sculpture. Examples include the other twelfth-century palmette fonts at Fowey, Lanlivery and Ladock, as well as the later medieval ones at Padstow and St Merryn. The crystal size is variable, but the medieval carvers preferred the finer variety.* Another greenstone that the Norman masons worked was Polyphant, quarried in the east of Cornwall near Launceston. Softer than Catacleuse, and flecked with pink crystals, it is still sought after by stonecarvers, though it doesn't weather well when placed outside.

Quarrying has always been hard and often dangerous work. At Beer in East Devon, the quarry was operational until the 1960s, with some blocks still extracted today under special licence. In the nineteenth century, a visitor described it as follows:

> The quarry … is entered by a gloomy archway, and extends, it's said, a quarter of a mile underground, at a depth of about 300 feet from the surface. The caves are both dark and wet, and form a mysterious labyrinth.

During the Second World War these conditions were entirely suited to its use as an explosives store, with munitions delivered by road and rail. Today, in the summer months, it is often open to the public but even on a hot July day it is a cold and dark place to visit, eerily quiet

---

* The Geological Survey concluded that for 'fine tooling and for standing weather no rock in Cornwall is better.'

despite the presence of other people, and, beyond the artificial lights, an intense black. A visitor could certainly be quickly lost.

Beer stone is a chalky, white, fine-grained limestone – and one of the best carving stones of the South West. It's a good stone for detailed work and hardens with exposure to the air. Many of the statues on the west front of Exeter Cathedral, carved in Beer stone in the 1340s, still show tool marks. The Romanesque masons used the stone for architectural pieces throughout Devon, including the fonts at Combeinteignhead and Buckland-in-the-Moor, the carved tympana at Down St Mary and Bishopsteignton, or the capitals and corbels at Hawkchurch, though it also occurs in pre-Conquest buildings such as the Saxon crypt at Sidbury St Giles and the Roman villa at Holcombe in East Devon.

I could hear the water far below, the eerie *thump thump* of waves echoing upwards from the base of the cliff. The sea glimmered silver in the sun. Fragments of stone peeped through the compacted earth of the coast path as it followed the steep gradients of the land. A quarry face and the remains of some associated workings, almost entirely overgrown with ivy and other greenery, appeared on one side of the path. A breeze rattled the exposed trees. I stopped to check my Ordnance Survey map. Polrudden Cove was close.

Of all the stones in the South West, the most unusual must be those found on the Lizard Peninsula in Cornwall. Geologists refer to this as an 'ophiolite sequence', a section of the Earth's oceanic crust that has been uplifted and exposed above sea level. The rocks here are metamorphosed, having been subjected to intense heat and pressure. It is possible to find gabbro, gneiss and serpentinite here. Faulting, in which large volumes of rock have shifted along particular planes, partial melting of rock, and alteration by circulating hydrothermal water, have all affected the area. It is a landscape of exposed heathland and unusual minerals. It is where the clergyman and geologist William Gregor discovered titanium in the late eighteenth century.

Serpentinite is the Lizard's famous stone. Found in a variety of marbled or banded colours from pale green to black and red, its relative softness means that it has been used for decorative and building work since the twelfth century. Polished serpentinite souvenirs of lighthouses or bowls, turned on a lathe, have been made and sold to tourists since the first factory opened at Poltesco in 1866. They still are, although there are fewer workshops today and a dwindling amount of the good carving stone left.

Up on the coast path the wind was beginning to bite. Dandelions and campion flowered in the sheltered spaces beneath the hedgerows. In places these hedgerows disappeared completely to reveal nothing but sky and cliff and white water troubling the rocks far below. The path continued to climb and twist and eventually allowed a view of Polrudden Cove, where the seam of Pentewan stone outcropped. It wasn't hard to find. A streak of pale gold cut the grey, a bright line painted across the face of the cliff.

A few days later I was in Sussex to visit my parents and my sister. My recent trip to Pentewan had got me thinking more closely about stones and their qualities, and in Hastings one afternoon, I was wondering why I might be drawn to some and not others. I was beginning to think that perhaps my judgements went far beyond the individual qualities of a particular stone; perhaps it was because of growing up here that some stones had unconsciously shaped my decisions. As I walked to the old town the sun was out, and so were the contents of many of the shops along the High Street, which were arranged in ramshackle and enticing displays. I was sidetracked by a row of books and then a box of postcards, principally because the one at the front was of Castle Drogo in Devon, the last castle in England to be built, its face somewhere between prison and palace, forbidding and vertical and sleek. And made of granite.

The postcard was an old one, probably 1960s. I bought it along with two others – three for ten pence. 'REFLECTS LIGHT' was scrawled in sloping capitals across the reverse of one of these, a photograph of a tribal mask. There were no details of the image at all, and the mask didn't look like it would reflect light – but at that moment, thinking of Castle Drogo as I was, the words made sense. Granite, grey and crystalline: reflects light. It's certainly true that on a bright day on Dartmoor the tors sparkle, the interlocking crystals of quartz, mica and feldspar grown slowly in deep batholiths of magma catching the sun. Is liking granite essential to finding happiness in the far South West? This is what the surrealist artist Ithell Colquhoun, who had left London for Lamorna in the late 1940s, once suggested. Perhaps she was right. I've always found it a difficult material to warm to, worked with great effort and weathering slowly – as the tall cliffs and moors suggest.

If I'd discovered that geology ceases to be an abstract science once you are holding a mallet and chisel, then I had also rekindled my relationship with stone but from a different perspective – as a material. It meant that I'd begun to favour certain stones over others based upon my experience of working them. From this I'd discovered a love for the Irish limestones from Connemara and Kilkenny, pale green and dark grey respectively; the chalk-like off-white limestone from Beer, soft to carve and able to hold a relatively good edge; the unusual 'marbles' (not true marbles but limestones that can be polished) of south Devon – Petitor, Ashburton, Pomphlett – with their vivid array of colours from pink to cream to black spiked with red or blue-grey.

On my way to Hastings Beach I stopped at a shop selling crystals and ornaments made from stones, and, in the attempt to try to understand the granites that the postcard had reminded me of, bought a small piece of quartz. The shop assistant wrapped it in tissue paper and put it into a turquoise bag. It was a hexagonal and asymmetrical crystal, clear at the naturally faceted end where different angled surfaces met in a point, cloudy at the other where it was broken off from its parent rock. I remembered its hardness was seven on the ten-point Mohs Scale, which meant it could scratch glass and was superseded only by topaz, corundum and diamond. It's the hardest mineral in the granite matrix, made of silica – the same as the flint pebbles that form much of the beach around here. My ambivalence towards granite comes I think from its toughness, but I'm not really sure. Perhaps it's something about its light-reflecting qualities – its ability to bounce back spectra that are beyond the range of my vision. Maybe, like some occult mirror, it reflects back everything, the totality of who you are; perhaps this is why the far South West can seem such a difficult place to live at times.

The sea was slate-grey below the sandstone cliffs. The tide was in but it looked like there was still enough beach to be able to sit by the wall at the far end of the car park. Every time I'm back in Sussex I head to the beach as soon as I can. I'm a beachcomber at heart, keen to follow the ridge of shingle pushed up by the last high tide to see what's been washed ashore. Beachcombing can be a kind of meditation if you want it to be, as it's easy to get lost among the shapes and shadows of the pebbles.

On that particular day the strand line was marked by clumps of bladderwrack, bleached cuttlefish bones, orange fishing twine, oyster shells. Driftwood is rare around here, but when it does turn up it can assume surprising forms. In the past I've found a turned chair leg, an entire tree, and a gingham-pattern table-top all within the space of a few hundred metres. I slid over the shingle ridges and found a place to sit with my back to the wall, a spot that offered a perfect view of the waves breaking over a spike of mussel-rich, black rocks.

The geology of this stretch of coast is unstable and shifts continuously. Sandstone underpinned by clay to the east, chalk threaded with bands of flint to the west. When it rains heavily there is a danger of cliff falls, the clay layer holding the moisture and making slippery contact with layers above. At Pett Level, just to the east of Hastings, abandoned houses perch precariously in the air, sections of wall hanging in the sky. A large proportion of Bulverhythe, which I'd just passed on the train, has disappeared in the last few centuries. At Birling Gap in the South Downs a run of cottages are being slowly eaten away. Here the porosity of the chalk cliffs proves irresistible to the hungry waves.

Unwrapping my recent purchase, I turned the crystal over in my hand. I have always been fascinated by how these natural objects can be so perfect, with clean lines and clear interiors, an entire other world. No wonder they so often bridge the gap between the real and legendary, from Merlin's crystal cave to the enchantress Melusine imprisoning her father inside a mountain. Crystals, stone, rocks: all suggest magical possibilities. One of the peculiarities of this stretch of coast from Bexhill to Hastings are holed stones, or 'hagstones'. These are nodules of flint in which the sea has found a point of weakness, usually a fossil coral or other creature, and worn a hole right through. Not only are you supposed to be able to see the faery kingdom if you look through the hole, but they are said to repel witches or 'hags'. Until the early twentieth century they were a common sight as an apotropaic totem, hung above windows and doorways in the county, often around stables too, or attached to the masts of fishing boats. The Sussex writer Cecile Woodford noted how they were used by healers to cure diseases, while their magical connections were appropriated by the occultist Aleister Crowley, who lived out his last years in Hastings. Local folklore says that he cursed the local residents to be doomed to return to the town unless they took a holed stone from the beach with them on their journeys.

Holed stones are a flint thing, and by virtue of that their folklore is connected to chalk regions: Sussex, Norfolk and so on. But really, all stones are closely identified with place. Think of the names: I carve a piece of Portland, or Beer, or Bath, rather than a generic limestone. In fact there is no generic limestone or generic any-kind-of-stone. Depending on which quarry it's from and which bed in that quarry, even the same stone will differ. Everything about stonemasonry goes against the contemporary drive towards homogenisation. Even making a geological map is an ambitious undertaking. Stones have character. This can't be mapped, but it can be apprehended, discovered, and to some degree, learned. Learning to work stone into a useful shape is not only a lesson in the qualities of that stone, but also a lesson in the qualities of that particular place, with something of that region absorbed, distilled, passed on – and at some level, understood.

A gull approached with an eye on my open bag, breaking my train of thought. I looked up, and after a brief stand-off it casually walked away. In the distance the power station at Dungeness gleamed in a patch of sunlight. This was the place that had seeped into my bones at the beginning: sandstone and clay, white chalk and black flint.

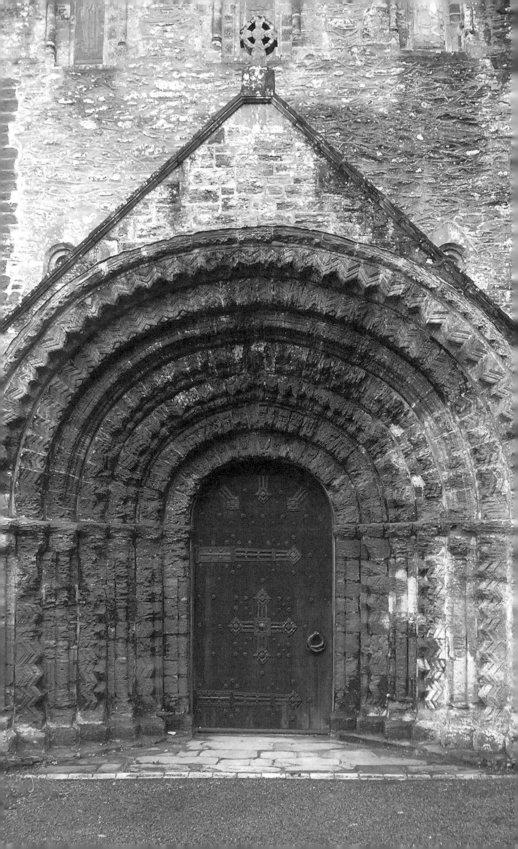

In Zigzag Shadow

Itook the train to St Germans. I was the only one to get off at the empty platform in the rain as comfortable passengers looked up from their phones and newspapers. I felt grateful that I had only a short walk to the church, at the edge of the Port Eliot estate in landscaped grounds next to an imposing manor house. As I walked down the gentle hairpin road to the entrance I felt like I was trespassing. I'd come to see the west portal, a gaping mouth of a doorway, composed of seven successively smaller arches (or 'orders') deep and animated by rows of zigzags. It seemed suitably overwhelming, particularly with a low, grey sky pressing an unexpected darkness into the stone, a coarse volcanic from Tartan Down near Landrake which varied in colour from deep green to mid-brown. The carving was flaky, friable and much had been lost. In places only the outlines of ghost chevrons meandered across raw lumps of stone; in others strong sharp points remained. It was a gap-toothed smile, ragged with age.

There is a whole glossary of chevron types. Common forms include the lateral chevron, where the design is carved parallel to the surface of the stone, and frontal, in which each point projects outwards at ninety degrees from the surface. 'Centrifugal' or 'centripetal' describes the direction of the 'V' upon the block of stone and in relation to the curve of an arch (Vs pointing outwards in the former, inwards with the latter). At St Germans Priory there were several different varieties grouped together in one extraordinary mass around the doorway. They loomed over me, the twisting lines of stone adding drama to what would otherwise be a plain entrance. Although they occur around plenty of doorways, few other sites in the South West, apart from the towers at Exeter Cathedral and the south door at Kilkhampton in north Cornwall, came close to this scale.

The west portal is just one aspect of this exceptional building, however. St Germans has been described as 'the most ambitious medieval church in Cornwall ... of impressive scale and design inside and out'. The twelfth-century remains include most of the west face of the church, the north and south towers, and the interior of the west end, including the beginnings of the south aisle arcade – a run of pointed arches supported by round columns with square, scalloped capitals. Beneath the towers, pilaster capitals are carved with scallop, volute, and other geometric designs.

The building that stands today began life between 1161 and 1184, when the Bishop of Exeter, Bartholomew Iscanus, re-established St Germans as a priory of Augustinian canons. According to tradition, St Germanus founded the first church in the early fifth century, although the earliest record documents Bishop Conan being invested here, nominated by King Athelstan in the 920s or 930s. St Germans was the cathedral of Anglo-Saxon Cornwall, with five bishops serving over about 120 years. As the seat of the bishops of Cornwall, St Germans was an important place, and had probably been an established monastery for several centuries prior to its reorganisation.

The rain was getting heavier so I headed inside to check my notebook. I was sure that Sedding had mentioned something about an unusual carving here, as I remembered writing it down, and sure enough, I eventually found it. 'The third capital from the west end of the nave,' he wrote, 'is embellished with grotesque figures having bodies resembling dogs, opposed to one another, with their fore parts meeting at the angle of the capital in one head, the upper part human, but the lower like a scallop shell.' I examined all the capitals in the nave as well as beneath the two west-end towers, but found nothing that fitted his description. It was one of Sedding's more puzzling comments. I looked again, just to make sure, but still nothing came close to this image. Had he imagined it?

The connection between St Germans Priory and Exeter Cathedral is significant. Work at Exeter started earlier than at St Germans, in 1114 under Bishop Warelwast, and was sufficiently advanced by 1133 for the building to be consecrated, though it was not completed until the very end of the twelfth or beginning of the thirteenth century. With the rest of the cathedral rebuilt in the Decorated Gothic style between about 1270 and 1350, the two towers at Exeter are the most substantial remains of its Romanesque past. During the late twelfth century, the upper levels of both were completed. It is possible that masons from Exeter also worked at St Germans, and perhaps vice versa, with sections and mouldings for ornament travelling between the two sites. On Exeter's north and south towers chevrons were used on a similarly large scale as those on the west portal at St Germans, the Norman masons placing them around blind arches, roundels or oculi, even along the edges of columns.

Cold and mindful of the limited train service from St Germans, I headed back to the station, reflecting on the austere geometric forms used to decorate this important building. Much of the carved stone inside was in such good condition and the lines so crisp it didn't look as if it were worked over eight hundred years ago. It could have been done last week. In some places, and this was one of them, Romanesque carving can look so new that you start to wonder whether it is genuine. It reminded me of a doorway that stood in the workshop at Weymouth College. This was no ordinary doorway, for it didn't lead anywhere – there was no opening, only the concrete wall against which it had been built. It was also a new Romanesque doorway. A perfect teaching tool: carved and built by the last intake of students and then, once the tutors had set to work with a hammer, mimicking a violent episode of weathering, repaired by them too. It looked odd, both old and new at the same time, a strange echo of the past jostling for space with the dust extractors and corrugated metal roofing. Not only was it an indicator of what might be expected of me, but it made me reflect on the persistence of the design. Did the stonemasons of the twelfth century ever wonder whether their work would last through the centuries? If they had, then this doorway would comfort their wandering ghosts. We were still making them, in order to learn how to repair them.

'There will be no free-carving on this course. Nobody, I repeat, nobody, will be "releasing the angel inside the stone" or whatever it is Michelangelo said. You'll carve according to a template or pre-arranged design. Is that clear?'

These were the first words spoken to us by our tutor Chris, who co-led the course at Weymouth College. It was September 2005. I wasn't sure I believed him. I had the feeling that most of us were here to do just that – to learn how to carve. I nodded solemnly, glancing around the workshop. Perhaps this wasn't the right thing for me after all. Or perhaps it was exactly the right thing. It was too early to tell. Chris was missing a finger. We were listening.

Two months earlier I'd attended an open day at the college. I'd spent years looking at stone carvings, but confronted with a working yard and the airy interior of the college workshop, I suddenly felt very out of place. Slabs of Portland stone were stacked outside. Carved stones were placed around the edges of the workshop, some of great complexity. A circular saw was in operation, slurry running out into the yard. At regular spaces there were work benches known as 'bankers' made of concrete blocks, some with work in progress by a current student upon them. I was looking for meaningful work. Was this it? Before I'd had too much time to think about it I was offered a place and immediately accepted.

In many respects it was a logical step because it didn't feel like I was ignoring my academic past. I'd found that my qualifications often counted against me when it came to finding work. In fact, I'd started leaving my degrees off my CV entirely, fudging the start and end date of jobs to cover the 'lost' years. In his book *The Case for Working with Your Hands*, the think-tank executive turned motorcycle mechanic, Matthew Crawford, suggests that academic accomplishments were now considered 'a poor basis on which to make hiring decisions', with many corporate, knowledge-based jobs 'not terribly demanding on the brain' or even requiring 'the active suppression of intelligence'. He argues that being able to think around a problem is less important, and certainly less dangerous to the order and hierarchy of most large companies, than 'fitting in'. As I'd discovered, these conditions of estranged labour were now commonplace.

Learning a craft can begin with a similar dissatisfaction. There are rules, and the material has its own ways and can be difficult to work. Yet this disillusion – 'the recognition that I am not what I thought I was, that I don't know what I thought I knew, that I can't do what I wish to do' – is nonetheless, as the potter Carla Needleman observes, 'the payment that opens us to the creative dialogue'.

What qualifications or experience did I have for practical work? Not much. At school I'd made a spice rack. It was fairly basic: three horizontals and two uprights, all in the same narrow pine board. The only concession to any decoration was a split dowel glued to the front of each vertical and a coat of varnish. Even by the standards of my classmates it was severe, and rather than the pursuit of any aesthetic vision, instead suggested its maker was interested only in minimal effort.

Then there was the metal coat hook. I'd snipped it out of sheet steel in the shape of a fish (I've no idea why) and then welded the hook, again cut in the same way, on to the front. I drilled two holes midway along the body of the fish, and then, in a final decorative flourish, enamelled the whole thing a bright lemon-yellow. It stood out, for all the wrong reasons.

Perhaps the highlight of these years was my electric-guitar clock, made out of Perspex. Modelled on James Hetfield of Metallica's angular and distinctive Gibson Explorer, it used only two colours: black and white. The main shape of the guitar was in white, glued and riveted onto a black circle, to give the hands of the clock something to follow. I used Letraset for the details of frets, pickups and so on, slotting the clock mechanism through a hole in the centre of the guitar body. I thought it was great. It also meant that my 'research' was largely reading *Kerrang!* magazine. It was fun and took no time at all, which meant that I could legitimately get away with not doing a great deal in class, though it paled in significance next to some of my far more ambitious classmates, some of whom were making cases for actual guitars.

My ham-fisted practicality continued down the years. In my twenties I started to make bookshelves out of wood salvaged from skips. In this I was encouraged by my then girlfriend Lou, who had a natural flair for construction and an eye for good design. Our carpentry was of the hammer-and-nails school and was usually carried out in the flat in the evening, once we were both back from our respective minimum-wage jobs. We would take apart pallets, remove the nails, and then use whatever wood we could salvage. Some evenings the flat looked like a working yard.

The turning point came when I started to make mosaics. What had begun as a hobby gradually become more and more complex as I realised just what was possible. I loved the colour and the vibrancy of the glass tiles early on, but then moved towards using the more muted colours of ceramic tiles. Essentially I was upcycling furniture: taking a found object like a broken table or cupboard, mending it and working a mosaic into it. When the design and the colour scheme worked, some pieces looked really good and I started to exhibit and occasionally sell them in a small gallery in Southampton.

This urge to make things but without really knowing how, was, by and large, how I came to the course in Weymouth: interested but uncertain, and by no means a natural. If the prospectus hadn't shown a photograph of a student smiling next to a slab on which he'd carved Romanesque-style star patterns, cable mouldings and other designs, I doubt I'd have applied. But I wanted to be able to do that, I knew and loved those designs too. Romanesque pattern pushed me onwards.

A few days before the course started, I found a place to rent on Rodwell Road in Weymouth. It was a quick bike ride downhill to the harbour, and through town to the college. My classmates were a mixed bunch. There were lads in their twenties, like Tom, Ben,

Wally and Pete, as I expected there would be, but I was pleased to find I wasn't the eldest student there nor that I was alone in having little practical stone-carving experience. Jemma had been a PA; Mimi a physiotherapist. Some were fleeing the dead ends of degrees that hadn't led anywhere; others were seeking a trade. There was an outlaw mentality that Chris, our tutor, fed by telling us stories about the good old days of conservation, when it was still possible to ride a Harley Davidson around the ruins of a castle.

The first exercise appeared simple enough: drawing an elevation of a building, to get us really looking at architectural details. I drew the west end of the church at Landscove in Devon. When you quietly look at a building, and I mean really just sit and look, something happens. You begin to notice things: a teardrop-shaped patch of algae below a broken downpipe; an asymmetrical roofline; traces of blocked-up doors or windows in the masonry. The building reveals different events in its life, which, if pieced together, will tell a story – perhaps different to the official one. A history of repairs, good ones and botched ones, of changing styles and fashions, of sometimes bizarre interventions. Differentiating between this palimpsest of styles or repairs is of course the basis of archaeology, with which I was familiar. But as I embarked upon a practical career, I realised that the ability to do so was an absolute necessity. Before you can begin to repair a building or a piece of stone you need to know what you're dealing with: what it is, how old it is and so on. Drawing is a good way into this, allowing your eye and your hand to find the shapes and patterns together.

Until I picked up a chisel I'd largely ignored geometric ornament in medieval sculpture. I was more interested in what I'd felt were the more engaging and immediate carvings of animals, monsters and humans. As I started working with my hands, however, I began to see these shapes more clearly. Romanesque decoration leans heavily on patterns, and the chevron stands out more than most. For something so simple it takes a bewildering variety of forms, adaptable as it is to almost any surface. The repetitive designs can cloak a wealth of nuances, and for those attuned to the later medieval period it is easy to dismiss these Romanesque zigzags as a simple, crude stepping stone on the path towards the adventurous Gothic. But to mistake directness of style for simplicity limits our appreciation, as it had mine. St Germans was an example of how, en masse, these patterns could create a unique sense of grandeur, whereas the font at West Chelborough in Dorset, also carved with geometric designs, revealed something else: the imperfect hand of its carver.

'We do good fonts around here. Have you been to Toller Fratrum?'
   'No,' I replied.
   'Ah, you'll like that, beautiful carving. What about Stoke Abbott?'
   'No, I've not visited that one either.'
   'You've got loads to go and see then! Don't forget Melbury Bubb. It's upside down and covered in strange animals.'
   A few days after my visit to St Germans I'd arranged to meet my friend John at his home in Dorset, so we could travel together to the village of West Chelborough. John is a stone carver with years of experience and a strong, distinctive style.

West Chelborough is in the heart of stone country, only a few miles from Ham Hill, which has been quarried for centuries, so perhaps it wasn't unusual to strike up conversations about the Romanesque with three strangers. Not that you need specialist knowledge. Often during my journeys I had discovered that the people who were the most passionate weren't experts but those who lived nearby or used the buildings on a regular basis, like the women we had met that morning. They were engaged with the building and the place, and because of this had wonderful local knowledge which they wanted to share.

But perhaps this generosity of spirit wasn't always evident. Wind the clock back a century and West Chelborough is described as 'a village so far from the haunts of men ... that the visit of a stranger causes some unrest'. This is what Frederick Treves wrote in his celebrated guidebook, *Highways and Byways in Dorset*, which was first published in 1906. Having gained fame and fortune as Royal Surgeon to Edward VII (operating on his appendix and saving his life just two days before the date of the King's coronation), Treves retired at fifty and turned his hand to writing – at this too he was a success, especially with *The Elephant Man* published in 1923.

To research *Highways and Byways*, Treves cycled over 2,000 miles around Dorset, which says much about his pioneering spirit: at the turn of the century, one of the most famous men in the British Empire was likely to be found pedalling along a rough chalk track deep in the countryside in order to visit remote stretches of coast and villages which were largely undisturbed.

Treves also described the country around West Chelborough as 'an undulating district of valleys and downs, of many trees, of deep lanes shut in by hedges so high that the narrow way is always in shade'. This is still the case over a hundred years later. As John and I neared the village, the roads twisted and the hedgerows blocked the view. Apart from the narrow slip of tarmac that quickly tapered to the next corner, everything was lit up with the prospect of imminent greenness, with adventurous buds and leaves brushing the sides of John's car. It felt like the road signs were deliberately primed to send the unwary around in circles – but then, suddenly, there was a bend in the road, the surface turned to gravel and there it was: a tiny church and a couple of houses. The lane was so narrow that parking the car against the hedge almost blocked the road. There was nobody around, and, at five o'clock on an overcast weekday, it was eerily quiet.

The church consisted of a chancel and a low tower attached to the south side of the nave, through which we entered. Although the font was right by the door I was immediately distracted by the huge and unusual monument attached to the north wall, an early seventeenth-century stone tomb, unusually without a date or dedication other than a coat of arms. There were two recumbent figures – a sleeping woman and child, tucked into a thick quilt – the whole piece carved by a tender hand.

The tomb is attributed to a highly successful stonemason of the period, William Arnold (*c.*1560–1637). In the early 1600s Arnold led an itinerant band of professional Somerset stonemasons who worked on a number of grand houses, of which Montacute in Somerset and Wadham College in Oxford are perhaps the most outstanding. Stonemasonry was in the Arnold blood. Born in the village of Charlton Musgrave to a mason who had worked on the rebuilding of Longleat House, Arnold's brother Godfrey was a stone sculptor, and at least one of his seven children followed him into the trade. Most of the men who worked with him came from families who lived close to the Ham stone quarries at Stoke-sub-Hamdon.

The font stood to the left of the door. Its passage through the last eight centuries had clearly been an eventful one, as there were chunks of stone missing here and there, some of the missing pieces about the size of my hand. But the carving was dazzling, the bands of ornament rising and falling, contracting and expanding, the decorative strips finding new slopes and gradients as they wound themselves around the bowl. Uppermost was a repeating pattern of leaves, bursts of three or four at a time that formed small palmette-like shapes; below this was cable ornament, the twists alternating between plain and beaded, the latter framed by thin lines; then wonderful, upright, rectangular stars; then shallow, saw-toothed-style chevrons; and at the base, a run of dogtooth, a kind of pyramidal star shape. Dogtooth would become a key motif in early Gothic sculpture, so its early appearance here suggested a date late in the Romanesque era, probably towards the end of the twelfth century.

These uneven bands of ornament were likely to be an accident of setting out (or lack of setting out) of the design, though it was far from unusual on Romanesque fonts. In many respects it added something to the work rather than detracted from it, bringing a warmth it might otherwise lack if everything were straight.

I like this about Romanesque sculpture – the quirks. Sedding liked it too, and sometimes wrote poetically about the traces of individuality he discovered. At the church of St James, Kilkhampton, on the north coast of Cornwall, he'd written a wonderful observation about a section of carving around the south door:

It may be observed in the illustration of the arch that the innermost ring is ornamented with 'heads and bird-beaks'. It should be noticed, however, that the sculptor has varied the usual formal ornament in three of the stones. Probably, during a pause in his work, he saw a bird carrying dried grass or straw to its nest, and so he conveyed the idea into his carving for ever.

Today, Sedding's 'bird-beaks' are called 'beakheads' and are distinguished by the presence of a bird's beak or a beast's snout, the heads to which they belong either human or animal, or, when it's hard to tell, maybe both. In this extract Sedding's whimsical origin for these 'bird-beaks' appears to draw on the fuzzier end of his Arts-and-Crafts background that romanticised direct copying from nature. But I wonder if he wasn't suggesting that, within the broader, fixed, schemes of decoration, the twelfth-century stonemason was an active participant, making decisions at each step that would affect the appearance of the finished piece.

It's odd how visiting one place can sometimes make you think very clearly about another, and as John and I took photos of the Arnold tomb and the font at West Chelborough I thought about the doorway at Kilkhampton, which I'd visited many years before. Perhaps it was because in this instance, Sedding was not the first writer on the scene (though he is the first to arrive there disgruntled, following a dismal walk from Bude station – 'five miles of almost perpetual uphill road' – and in 'such a wind-swept district as this'.) James Hervey, the philosopher, poet and rector, is understood to have drawn on the atmospheric surroundings of the church when composing his influential *Meditations Among the Tombs*, first published in the mid-eighteenth century. One of the 'graveyard school' of poets, Hervey would become enormously popular, inspiring Horace Walpole's *Castle of Otranto*, and, indirectly, the entire Gothic Revival.

Kilkhampton's Romanesque south doorway is a monumental one. Hervey described it as 'peculiarly rich and beautiful … enriched with grotesque heads and several bands of zigzag sculpture'. The beakhead motif in the South West of England is rare, found for the most part in the counties of Oxfordshire and Yorkshire. In Cornwall, other than at Kilkhampton, it occurs around the south door and on one arch of the north nave arcade at Morwenstow, as an individual corbel at Mylor, and just across the border in Devon at Shebbear, Buckland Brewer, Woolsery and Bishopsteignton. This pocket of Cornish and Devonian beakhead has intrigued me for a while. The art historian Ron Baxter writes that it is 'unsuspected links of patronage' which can throw up surprisingly rich displays of beakhead ornament 'in counties that are otherwise lacking in the motif'; this would certainly make sense here. But what was going on in this part of north Cornwall in the mid-twelfth century to warrant the appearance of such a complex and advanced piece of work?

The origin of the beakhead motif in England is usually taken as Reading Abbey in Berkshire, founded by Henry I as his mausoleum in 1121. The connection with Henry I is a significant one. In the years following his death in 1135, Cornwall became an arena in which two of his illegitimate sons built their power bases. One of them, Robert of Gloucester, owned the manor of Kilkhampton.

Robert of Gloucester is a standout figure in the landscape of twelfth-century history. A patron of the arts and letters and a politician of 'proved talent and admirable wisdom', as the anonymous author of the *Gesta Stephani* noted in the late 1140s, he had 'all the kingly attributes except one: legitimacy'. His architectural ambitions are clear in what remains of the Priory of St James in Bristol, which was established by him in 1129 and is an early, unusual example in the Romanesque architecture of the South West. It would be unusual, given his connections with Kilkhampton during this period, if he weren't involved with the sudden appearance of this dramatic and high-status doorway with its display of architecturally advanced motifs in an otherwise remote village. My feeling is that it is through him that the beakhead motif is likely to have come to Cornwall. The doorway itself may reflect Robert's attempts, perhaps, to emulate his father's ambitious programmes of art.

At Kilkhampton the four orders of chevron and beakhead, carved columns and capitals use scale and repetition to draw attention to the entrance to the church. On such a grand doorway it's easy to miss the lovely secret highlight of the work: a tiny head with its tongue poking out that can be found squeezed into the end of a run of chevrons on the east side. No bigger than two inches across, this

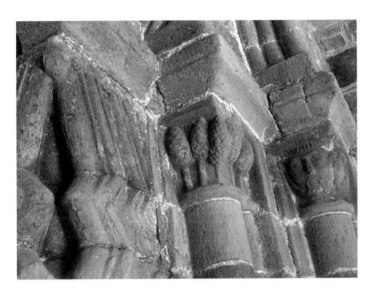

head's been sticking out its tongue to the curious and unwary for several centuries. Throughout much of the twentieth century scholars of medieval carving had written about the 'unlearned' stonemasons who, to many of them, seemed concerned only with attempting to insert jokes into their work. I think that such an interpretation is a bit demeaning My feeling is that they understood these buildings well – they *had* built them – and that such details were more a way of humanising an awesome and overwhelming structure, of giving it a sense of life that geometric ornament alone could not.

This flexibility of motifs is often overlooked but it is the key to the success of Romanesque sculpture. I started to think about other places where the stonemasons had taken it to new levels, and naturally, with my mind on the north coast of Cornwall as it was, my thoughts turned to the mesmerising and otherworldly church at Morwenstow.

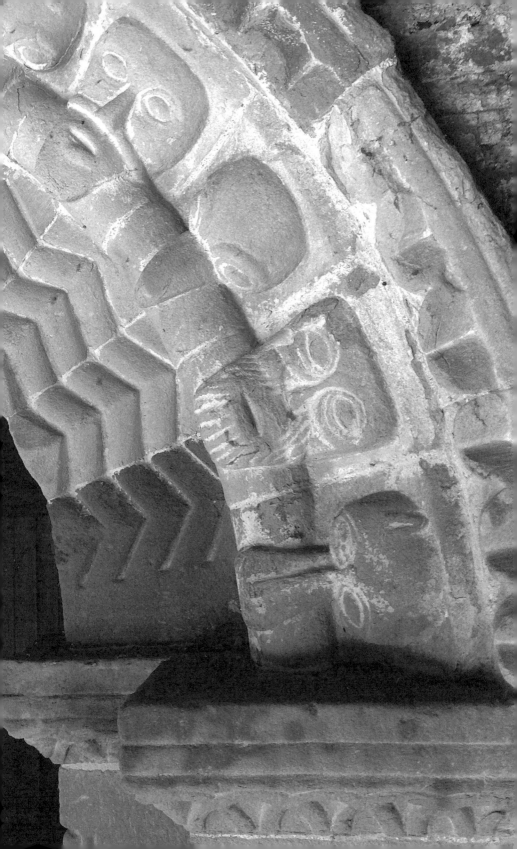

Beakheads at Morwenstow

'Did you know Rose, two doors down from us, is a hundred years old?' said a man three seats in front of me. I was on the branch line from Exeter to Barnstaple, a copy of J. R. A. Hockin's *Walking in Cornwall* open on the table in front of me. There was a tangible sense of going back in time. The train appeared to be one for enthusiasts, and judging by its square and unfamiliar shape looked like it entered service in the 1960s (though I'd been told by a man with a camera around his neck it was the 1980s); the line itself, with its evocative and silent stations – Morchard Bishop, Eggesford, Umberleigh – twisting its way past solitary houses and abandoned barns. The sky was overcast and the animals dotted throughout nearby fields looked up as our carriages disturbed the emptiness, startled ones running away and spreading the panic to their companions. 'She doesn't look it,' the woman eventually replied to her companion, but my eavesdropping was suddenly curtailed by a shift in gear that rendered all communication useless, the diesel engine reaching deafening frequencies with the increase in speed.

I returned to my book. I'd brought Hockin's guide with me despite having no intention of walking anywhere in Cornwall. My plan was to pick up the 319 bus from Barnstaple which would take me to Hartland via Bideford, Woolsery post office and Clovelly visitor centre (among other places) in one hour and twenty-three minutes – if the timetable was to be believed. But Hockin is sensitive to landscape, and although he is describing Cornwall when he writes about the 'hair-raising grimness' of the north coast near Morwenstow, he is right to observe that the nearby county boundary with Devon is 'purely arbitrary', and that the area around Hartland is its own 'mysterious and separate region'.

Hockin's book was first published in 1936 and was reprinted several times throughout the following decades. Like the antiquarian Richard Pearse Chope, who wrote that Hartland before the Great War 'was almost isolated from the world outside', Hockin understood the importance of the unique situation of the village, bounded on two sides by the sea and on the other two by deep valleys. As Chope, who lived in Hartland, pointed out, it was on the road to nowhere, 'sufficiently forbidding to many people' and 'farthest from railways', an unknown country to all but 'a few adventurous persons'. An ideal location, then, for a reclusive religious community, and no doubt part of the reason behind Hartland Abbey being the last in England to be dissolved by Henry VIII, in 1539.

At Barnstaple terminus I crossed the bridge over the River Taw to the bus station. Drizzle pushed in from the coast, adding an unexpected chill. The single-decker was parked up, empty, so I sat and waited on a sheltered bench nearby.

People come here to escape. If the Augustinians had pioneered this in the twelfth century, renouncing the world in pursuit of things spiritual, then it seemed a good path to follow in the early twenty-first century as well – though for different reasons. It had been a while since I'd lived in north Devon, and as I waited for the bus, I thought back to those days and how they'd begun.

It was March 2003 when I left my house in Heatherdene Road in Southampton clutching a cardboard box, my destination the arts campus of the university at the end of the road. The box contained three hardbound copies of my thesis, each one, with appendices, 120,000 words. It represented three and a half years of my life, three and a half years in which my mind had hummed twenty-four hours a day with a research project. Watching the television I'd be thinking about stone sculpture; going to sleep I'd have to get up to write something down; cycling across the common I'd stop and scribble something into a notebook. A comment might spark a connection or a realisation, which, in combination with my loose approach towards planning (how can you plan something you haven't yet found out?) meant that I was continually rewriting, discarding, editing, researching, writing. My ways often perplexed or infuriated my supervisor, but then that is the life of the research student. The more you find out the more there is to discover.

Writing the thesis had led to moments where I'd felt truly connected to something. This wasn't just to the material, the nuts and bolts of my subject, but something far beyond that. Reading long-gone writers on the subject and getting to grips with their arguments, balancing them against current theories and my own ideas was like entering into a conversation in which both the dead and the living participated. It felt incredible to be part of this centuries-long enquiry, in which medieval sculpture was a springboard into other ideas and worlds.

Even better, I was in love. Theresa was writing her PhD on medieval sculpture too. As the only two doctoral students in the department writing about medieval art there was a sense of inevitability about our eventual meeting up, but it turned out we had more in common than archaeology. Her lightning mind and unconventional approach to research and, indeed, life, lit up my world, and after a while she and her young daughter moved into the house I'd previously shared with other postgraduates in Heatherdene Road.

When I ran out of funding I became a postman, starting my days cycling across a deserted wintry city to the depot and finishing them later on in the stifling warmth of the Hartley Library, surrounded by my notes, fighting to stay awake. Writing inevitably slowed, but out of the chaos a coherent piece of work finally emerged, and a few months later I was ready to hand it in. I was pleased – it was an original contribution to the subject – but I didn't feel any joy at having completed it. In many respects I didn't want to hand it over. As I plonked the box onto the desk in the postgrad office, signed the paperwork to confirm that it was my own work, I felt a part of my brain that had been spinning for the last few years tip ever so slightly off its axis.

We'd been visiting Devon on and off for a while before Theresa's Mum died; but when she did her house in Torrington became our home as we sorted out her belongings. As the roadside sign declared, Torrington was a 'Cavalier Town', a reference to its loyalty to the Crown during the Civil War rather than the devil-may-care attitude of its inhabitants. Nonetheless it never failed to amuse us, and gradually it became a relief to see it. Southampton to Torrington: we had escaped. But escape, it turns out, isn't that easy. I'd lived in urban settings all my life. Torrington, a small town in the agricultural landscape of north Devon, demanded new skills. Now I had a grieving partner, a small child to help look after, a new environment to get to grips with, a brain that felt it was in perpetual fog, no nearby friends, no income, and no PhD to distract me from it all.

Instead there was Appledore, Bideford, Northam, Clovelly, Hartland, Horwood. Sand and salt, fields bleached by the sun. Earth and water defined this landscape. The land, spectacularly resistant to the passing of time, hugged pockets of houses to itself, white paint and slate roofs peeping from its bends and folds and gradients. In July, water trickled along gullies and ditches. In November sheets of it blinded roads – the fields sloughed it off like a beast emerging from the deep for air. After Southampton it was a paradise of winter mud and bruising weather.

I started to visit some of the nearby churches. It didn't matter that I couldn't feel anything, or that I feared that I'd lost a part of myself for good. The centuries-old buildings welcomed me, and my habit of seeking out bits of Romanesque and Gothic sculpture had been so ingrained by my studies by this point that I carried on. I didn't know it at the time, and even later refused to take on board what the GP was telling me. I wasn't the kind of person to have depression. It wasn't for me. It was something that other people had. But whatever I thought didn't matter: it was there, flowering like knotweed in the clean air and claustrophobic hedgerows.

★

The driver appeared and the bus rattled into life. Like most vehicles that have survived a winter on the roads of north Devon it was covered with a fine brown spray, a mixture of the runoff from fields glazed and semi-crystallised with grit-salt. Muted in this way, the bright colours of the company's logo no longer stood out, giving the bus an agricultural appearance. It was a relaxed service. As we pulled out of Barnstaple and headed towards Bideford, a woman a few seats in front of me unwrapped a sandwich and poured herself a black coffee from a flask. The other two passengers were silent, surrounded by shopping bags, quietened by the engine rhythms and occasional squeal of brakes.

My intention for this trip, first and foremost, was to see the font at Hartland. It was an added bonus to be able to sit on the bus for an hour or so absorbed in the landscape outside. I smiled to myself: for the last few days, on and off, I'd been reading Hockin's book, which was all about walking, and here I was, a passenger on a vehicle – exactly the thing he'd been against. I felt like a bit of a fraud until I remembered that in a landscape where the roads are narrow and the hedges high, any elevation is useful. It can be surprising how a glimpse over a hedge might reveal a building or a view impossible by any other means.

It has been said that Devon as a whole is 'not especially rich in Romanesque architectural sculpture'. This, however, isn't true, though it might appear that way at first glance. Pieces of work are spread thinly across a vast territory and there are few standout sites where it survives in any concentration, though they do exist at Hawkchurch and Bishopsteignton, for instance. Perhaps not quite as sculpturally rich as more famous sites such as Kilpeck in Herefordshire or Barfreston in Kent, these places nonetheless deserve to be on the map. On doorways, fonts, and in other fragments in the north of the county, as well as at Kilkhampton and Morwenstow in north Cornwall, a highly recognisable style suggests the presence of a successful workshop in the region during the mid-twelfth century.

The doorways at Shebbear, Woolsery and Buckland Brewer are the best known. Each one is almost identical, suggesting a kind of twelfth-century production line: an inner order of a chevron repeated three times, then an arch of beakheads, and then, on the outermost arch, a strange geometric motif resembling a cut cylinder, the two halves angled like the wings of a resting butterfly. The beakheads are themselves repeated forms composed of four types: a bird head; an animal head with a long-ridged snout and folded triangular ears; a human head with a moustache; and an occasional human head with pointed animal ears on the top of the skull.

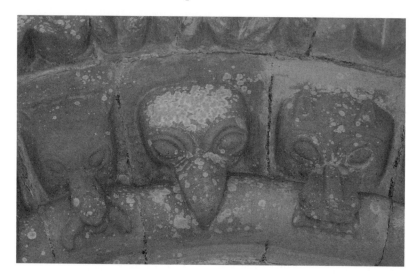

Of all of these there is the most variation in the animal heads, but across the whole range of the imagery, even those that at first glance appear identical, no two designs are exactly the same. Sometimes the beasts grip something in their mouths, as they do at Shebbear. At Buckland Brewer the human heads taper into pointed chins. At Parkham there is just one beakhead, a face at the apex of the arch. These decorated arches rest upon capitals carved with top-heavy volutes, the abaci above them cut with intersecting semicircles. This standard template does indeed suggest that the individual stones of these doorways were mass produced, probably off-site, and then delivered to the churches for assembly.

The most striking of the group is the doorway at Shebbear. This appears as a muddle of Romanesque and Gothic, the inner order with its chevron decoration trimmed into a pointed arch. In all other respects, though, the sculpture of the doorway remains similar to the others, with the flat chevron and outer geometric ornament framing the plain roll moulding of the central order.

In the wider context of later Romanesque sculpture in Devon, the work of the north finds few parallels. Late-twelfth-century work at Exeter Cathedral hasn't survived in anywhere near as good condition as the north Devon carvings, and what does remain suggests a substantially different aesthetic. In the cathedral, heads of both humans and animals are carved with large eyes, triangular noses and grinning or closed mouths. While most are now too weathered for any appreciation of detail, a carved corbel reused in the building of the Chapel of St James, discovered after the chapel's destruction by a German bomb in 1942, illustrates the genre well. In this example the large eyes are punctured with drilled pupils and there is a toothy grin for a mouth, much like those at Plympton, on the outskirts of Plymouth, with which many of the north and south tower examples at Exeter share a close affinity.

I'd first discovered these works through an article published in 1957 by two eminent scholars, François Henry and George Zarnecki. It was called 'Romanesque Arches Decorated with Human and Animal Heads'. Their research on medieval churches on the continent and in Britain and Ireland enabled them to plot the whereabouts of Romanesque arches, typically doorways, that featured beakheads. As their map showed, in England these decorated doorways were concentrated in Yorkshire and Oxfordshire. But there were tantalising outposts and this was one of them, in north Devon and north Cornwall, a little cluster of dots surrounded by blank space. I'd been intrigued, and as I was living nearby started to seek them out, usually by bike, cycling into headwinds and blinding sun on roads without signs that weaved through dense hedgerows and up formidable inclines. It must be some of the most overlooked sculpture in Britain, hidden in weathered churches that themselves hid among farmland and high pale skies, a spectral presence in the archaeological literature.

At the centre of it all was Hartland Abbey. Built in 1157 and consecrated three years later by the Bishop of Exeter, Hartland was built on a pre-Norman foundation. Within a decade it was re-established as a house of Augustinian canons (in 1169) and new building work was underway by 1171. The abbey buildings were located in a sheltered valley some distance from the site of the church, and after the Dissolution the former abbot's lodgings were converted into a house. It is a beautiful place to visit, especially on a spring day, when snowdrops and primroses carpet the wooded valley slopes and the leafless trees stand motionless in the coastal air.

Out of Bideford, the roads were drying out, creating a patchwork of lights and darks on the tarmac. Rogue daffodils splashed their rich yellow beneath the impenetrable hedges. I recognised these twists and turns in the roads. The tower of the church of St Nectan, the tallest in north Devon at 128 feet, appeared in the distance only to disappear again as the gradient shifted beneath our wheels. I knew that, not far off, the grey cliffs of Hartland Point climbed out of white water, monumental sections of slate themselves folded into waves, syncline and anticline, by earth movements millions of years ago.

I love how isolated and secret this part of the world always seems. Chope was right: the difficulty of getting here nourishes a sense of otherworldliness. We travelled through the village, then out towards the coast. The huge tower of the church came into view once again. I asked to be dropped off nearby, and soon enough found myself standing outside the gate to the churchyard as the noise of the engine faded. I had about two hours before the return journey.

I'd forgotten the enormous size of this building, which seemed to bear no relation to its immediate location. If anything, it appeared more attached to the sky than to the earth, the fields and hedgerows doing little to hold it in any conventional perspective. The same was true for the inside, a cavernous interior filled with treasures. These included a fifteenth-century chest tomb carved from Catacleuse stone, one of the best pieces of Devon's later medieval sculpture, rich with tracery and repeated quatrefoils; the wooden screen of the same period, still bearing traces of original paint; a small room above the north porch crammed with all manner of stone fragments and oddities including a seventeenth-century organ; a plaque to the memory of Penguin Books founder Allen Lane, who lived nearby; some twentieth-century roof bosses, carved in wood and difficult to make out in the gloom, one of them a mermaid.

The font was hard to ignore, a giant golden-coloured square thing carved with repeating and eye-catching patterns, the stone a fine-grained volcanic, its two massive sections, identically shaped, joined together mid-pedestal. Around the top of the square bowl were characteristic intersecting semicircles in different sizes and designs. Interspersed with triplets of beading, they radiated outwards from the centre around the base too. On the corners of both sections, base and top, were human heads with slender moustaches, each one staring at its counterpart. It was immediately recognisable as work

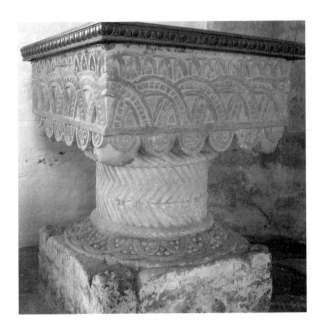

of the later twelfth century from this part of the world. I made a few notes and tried to take a reasonable photo, though the darkness, even with the lights on, lent it an ancient texture that looked out of place on my phone's screen.

My time was nearly up. There was a small collection of secondhand books for sale by the door, all of them fifty pence each. I noticed an edition of *Cornwall: England's Farthest South*, by the journalist Arthur Mee, its distinctive dark-blue dust jacket torn at the edges and the pages wavy from damp. I dropped some coins in the box and put it in my bag. Settling in for the bus journey back to Barnstaple, I started reading it and was perplexed by what he wrote about Morwenstow, just over the county boundary in north Cornwall:

> It is a magnificent doorway which leads us into this fine church with four orders of Norman carving. It has a string of roses held up by two queer animals, a dragon crouching in the presence of a lamb, a mermaid and a dolphin and a whale, all worked into an arch held up on two small piers with fine capitals.

A mermaid and a dolphin and a whale? I'd been to Morwenstow several times and was sure I'd have remembered such unusual carvings. Like Sedding, I'd even sat and drawn some of the sculpture on occasion. I pulled one of the many notebooks I'd brought with me out of my bag, one in which I'd gathered together some photos and sketches of the churches in the area, but could find nothing of that description. Perhaps Mee's sea creatures had weathered between the 1930s, when he was writing, and the early 2000s when I'd taken the photos – certainly there were a couple of indecipherable lumps of stone that once were carved with something. But the general pattern around the doorway was decorative bosses and the occasional flower or beast head, nothing that would suggest the presence of a mermaid or anything equally exotic.

It was interesting to be reminded of the church of St Morwenna at Morwenstow again. One of the 'most atmospheric of churches', according to Pevsner, owing in large part to its scenic position, tucked into the slope of a steep valley, only a field or two from a sheer drop into the Atlantic. It's also the richest site in Cornwall for Romanesque sculpture. Sedding, too, was struck by the 'wild situation of this most charming sanctuary', and spent many hours drawing the work there.

St Morwenna contains two distinct phases of work from the twelfth century, the earliest of which is around the south doorway and porch. This doorway was moved from its original position when the south aisle was added in the sixteenth century. When this happened it was split into two parts. The outermost arch went to form the entrance to the porch, while the remaining two orders and the residual columns and capitals of the absent arch formed the doorway to the main body of the church. It is here that the bulk of the decoration is to be found, a dizzying array of chevron and beakhead. The capitals are carved with stylised foliage, a heavily eroded double-bodied beast and a spray of pinecone-like seed heads. On the apex of the porch outside there are carved beasts supporting the Agnus Dei on a rope, the ends of which are held in each creature's mouth. There are corbels on the exterior of the porch too, isolated survivals of a highly idiosyncratic style: beast masks with enormous eyes and mouths slashed across the entire width of the head.

The later sculpture is inside, on the north arcade. Chevrons, bosses, beakheads and geometric designs are carefully ordered around the arches, and there are heads of animals and humans set where the arches meet. This is where Mee, not content with his mermaid on the south porch, suggested that there was a carving of a hippo. It's difficult to substantiate, which is a shame: though I can see, with one carving in particular, where he might have got his idea from. At the eastern end of the arcade, the abacus to the capital is delicately carved with rosette motifs and interlaced semicircles, the latter very similar to those on the font at Hartland or on the abaci at Buckland Brewer, Parkham, Woolsery or the tympanum at Bondleigh. You can understand why Mee believed these arches were the finest in Cornwall and among the best in England. If the Romanesque work of the region took root in Kilkhampton, kick-started by the patronage of Robert of Gloucester, then developed under the expansion of Hartland Abbey, it reached its fullest expression back in Cornwall in this arcade.

The chronology seems to be this: the south doors at Kilkhampton and Morwenstow appear first, and date to the 1130s or 40s. The close similarities between the two, not only in the arrangement and style of the beakheads and voussoirs, but in the shared, and unusual motif of pinecones or hops that are carved on capitals at each church, suggest that Robert of Gloucester's masons worked at both sites. The addition of an aisle was the usual means of enlarging a church in the medieval period, so the building of the north aisle and associated nave arcade at Morwenstow is a later event. This dates to the period when the north Devon stonemasons were producing work, so is likely to have taken place somewhere between 1150 and 1180, the period when Hartland Abbey was re-established. The sculpture associated with this phase of building takes a new turn, with chevrons carved in threes and the appearance of particular geometric accompaniments such as the split cylinder motif, volutes and intersecting semicircles.

The quality of the work at Morwenstow hasn't always found a happy home among the county's literature. In his bestselling *England's Thousand Best Churches*, Simon Jenkins briefly describes the Romanesque work here, noting the 'Norman beasts' of the south door before touching upon the survival of the Norman north arcade: 'green, damp and primitive'. The stone of the south door is often covered with green algae but not the work inside, which usually appears disarmingly fresh, almost as if it's been carved in the last year as opposed to the last eight hundred. And is it primitive?

It has been argued that the invention of Cornwall as a tourist destination over the last century has promoted romanticised notions of the county as 'a place of retreat, simplicity and innocence, peopled by bucolic, smiling villagers'. This idea, coupled with the severity and natural beauty of the landscape, has been an alluring one, but it is also what feeds the idea of 'primitivism'. Certainly at Morwenstow there is a sense of the primitive in the masks and beaks, the staring, blank eyes and the repeated geometric forms. The Romanesque in Cornwall draws out these assumptions: in a 'rugged' landscape perhaps we expect 'primitive' art. But this doesn't mean they are crude – which is implied in his reading – and herein lies the problem. Primitive is generally defined in negative terms, lacking in refinement or technological accomplishment, suggesting something 'less complex, or less advanced' than something else. Just as the sophisticated and thoughtful forms of the Romanian sculptor Constantin Brancusi (1876–1957) were often derided as primitive, so Romanesque sculpture – which shares much with modernist artists – can be easily overlooked. But from my own experience carving stone I know that mistakes are easier to hide in highly decorative and ornamental work than among straight lines, simple curves and flat surfaces. In fact, you could say that 'primitive' is actually quite difficult in practice – to achieve the balance between a sense of life in the work and the technical skill of producing the work in the first place isn't straightforward, and can only come with time. As I had discovered first-hand at Weymouth.

My great-great-great-great-great-great-great-grandfather Alexander Farquharson was born in Aberdeenshire in 1716, grew up surrounded by the moorlands and forests on the south side of the River Dee, married a local girl, Margaret Davie, with whom he had seven children, and became the third and last Laird of Balfour, his executors selling the five- to six-hundred-acre estate to the Earl of Aboyne after his death in 1791. The estate was new to this branch of the Farquharsons, only in the family for three generations, a total of 132 years, his grandfather Donald having obtained it in 1659. Alexander was a stonemason.

Geoffrey Farquharson, author of *Clan Farquharson*, writes that the reason the estate was sold was to prevent Alexander's eldest son Francis (nicknamed 'The Buck of Birse' for his extravagant habits) from inheriting it. But I've also read that Alexander mismanaged the estate because he was an alcoholic. In his defence, drinking was a daily hazard of stonemasonry before effective dust extraction. As Seamus Murphy recounts in *Stone Mad*, his lively account of being an apprentice stonemason in Ireland during the 1920s, the feverish thirst worked up by the carvers meant that one of his crucial tasks was to collect the morning beer, a position he occupied 'for about four years until I was relieved by another apprentice'. Murphy was writing about life in the early twentieth century but thirsty work remains thirsty work, and traditions are surely passed on from somewhere.

In 1814, twenty-three years after his death, William, Alexander's second son, set up a memorial to his father in the cemetery at Birse.

It is a fitting piece of work to commemorate a stonemason: a white marble tabletop slab cut with well-shaped letters, supported by two upright pieces of stone with simple capitals carved at each end.

This Alexander, discovered through doing some genealogical research online, was an important find for me. I had, after all, some connection to the craft, some stony DNA passed on. My choice to go and learn it perhaps wasn't so out of the blue after all: I was continuing a family trade, though one broken by a couple of centuries. As I struggled to pick up the basics on my course I thought of him more and more. Had he ended his days as an alcoholic, or was it just a distortion of history and a consequence of hard work in an unforgiving environment? I didn't know. But I was aware and proud of an inheritance of sorts, and hoped I could draw upon it, however subtle it may be, in my own work.

Learning to carve a flat surface was perhaps where I needed Alexander's guiding hand the most. An essential skill, it underpins pretty much everything a stonemason will be expected to do, and, to begin with at least, sounded straightforward. To start the process of learning it we had, on one particular day back at Weymouth, been given freshly sawn blocks of Portland limestone, each face perfect. But then something unexpected started to happen. Our tutor, Chris, with barely suppressed, childlike glee, wandered from banker to banker with a pitching chisel and lump hammer, breaking away enormous pieces of stone from our blocks. A sense of unease ran through me.

The pitching chisel or pitching tool is the only one in the kit without a cutting edge; instead it has an angled face about five millimetres deep which, when placed against the side of a piece of stone and struck with a hammer directs a shockwave leading to the removal – sometimes in dramatic fashion – of large chunks. In the sequence of tool use it is the first, its job to get rid of waste as quickly as possible. On this particular day, the 'waste' was the top of our regular blocks, which, after a few seconds of Chris's attention, were now battered and broken. Our lesson was to work this back to a new flat surface.

The technique is known as 'boning in'. It allows an irregular lump fresh out of the quarry to be turned into a usable ashlar block with little more than a straight edge, a level, a square, some equal-sized cubes of wood and a handful of chisels. You begin with a small corner, carefully cutting enough room on which to sit one of the cubes, making sure as you gently advance into the stone that the surface is level (and, if you're lucky enough to have a nearby right-angled face, also square). This is repeated on the next corner, only now a level is balanced between the two, propped upon the cubes so that it clears the irregular stone between. Once this is true you repeat the process on the remaining two corners, checking as you do that each is level with the others.

When these little corners are complete, a line can be scribed into the edge of the stone to connect each one and a draft worked in. This will leave you with a kind of 'picture frame', a chisel-width flat surface around the edge of the stone. The mass left behind in the middle then has to be worked down (using a punch, then a claw, then a boaster chisel) and if nothing goes wrong and you've not dipped under the line, what is left is a beautiful hand-tooled flat surface.

Easy enough, you might think. But with each attempt something new presented itself, something previously unconsidered. Fossils would need careful attention so as not to pop out and leave an indentation. Shell fragments had to be approached similarly. The fear of undercutting also seized many of us, which led to tentative working. After many attempts and restarts and hours lost to the task Chris finally gave me the nod, but it might have simply been expedient to do so. I'd taken the stone down so many times it was virtually a paving slab.

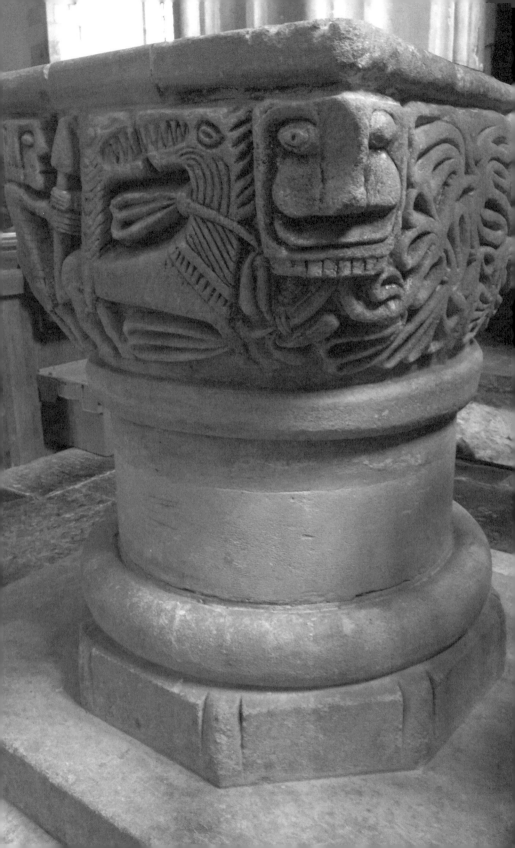

Four Fonts

'Use any stone you like, apart from the marble and this bit here: I've got plans for that.' I was in John's workshop at his house in Poole. I'd been here before, but this time was different: he'd asked me to look after the house while he and his wife Monique were on holiday, so I was getting a full tour. Naturally, though, we'd lingered among the stones, tool cabinets and bankers, under the clear corrugated plastic roof that marked out this space between the house and the garage as a working one.

John, like me and probably most other stonemasons, is a hoarder of stones, which means he's always keen to see offcuts used up – especially with the house on the market and plans for moving in progress. In the workshop, rooting around beside the many repurposed cupboards and shelves, I found some triangular pieces of Portland, waste pieces from an earlier project. I liked the shape and thought that I'd be able to squeeze something into that space, as the medieval carvers often did on irregular architectural features. Whiling away the time on the train journey to John and Monique's, I'd been doodling some designs in my notebook. Now it occurred to me that these triangles might be perfect for one of them, a mermaid with a crooked tail, like the wonderful carving on the wooden bench in the church at Zennor in Cornwall.

It felt strange to be occupying someone else's house, but I set to work once John and Monique had left and soon the familiarity of working stone helped me to feel more comfortable. By mid-afternoon, with the sun shining directly into the workshop, flattening the light and making it almost impossible to read the depths of cut, I stopped to eat a late lunch in the garden. I thought back to an earlier conversation I'd had with John, just before he left, about a handful of fonts in the area that I'd yet to see. Toller Fratrum, Stoke Canon, Luppitt, Dunkeswell: the names sounded like an incantation or a spell. John and I had planned to visit Luppitt and Dunkeswell together when they were back from their holiday; Stoke Canon I could do from Exeter next time I was there. This left only Toller Fratrum in west Dorset.

I finished my lunch and looked down from the top of the sloping garden to the workshop. I could just about make out the rough outline of the mermaid I'd spent the morning blocking out. Its jagged shape seemed like a small accomplishment for the hours I'd spent on it so far. But something was emerging nonetheless.

Around the time I was house-sitting for John and Monique, I'd started to read Pevsner's *Buildings of England* series again. Years ago, I'd found his general distaste for the Romanesque unpalatable. But I'd been lured back by a discount offered by Yale University Press, the publisher of the series, and I soon found myself collecting the early editions whenever I saw them in secondhand bookshops. Gradually, I was won over by the sheer volume and astonishing variety of buildings that I knew nothing about.

I remained wary, though. Pick up the Devon edition of Pevsner and look for descriptions of the Romanesque fonts of the county and you will find that the following descriptions appear, some more than once: 'barbaric' (Luppitt), 'carved in the most elementary style' (Stoke Canon), 'very crude craftsmanship' (Dunkeswell), 'the meaning not clear' (South Milton). These comments mask the fact that Devon's Romanesque fonts represent some of the artistic highlights of the county. There's an astonishing number of fonts left – 186 are listed in the five-volume catalogue compiled by Exeter University student Christina Corser. When you consider their age and their often atrocious post-medieval histories in which many were abandoned, buried, or smashed into fragments (sometimes all three), this is quite something.

Perhaps Pevsner can be read as a kind of collective emotional response, a moral index of aesthetics, crystallising all the cultural prejudice that others have felt about them over the last few centuries. Not everyone, though, has recoiled from these works. Some, such as the artist John Piper (1903–1992), have been crucial in recognising the value of Romanesque sculpture. Indeed, it was because of him that the church of St Basil at Toller Fratrum was on my list.

Throughout his life, Piper photographed buildings, landscapes and medieval architecture and sculpture in England, creating an extraordinary archive of photographs which are now held at the Tate. Numerous atmospheric images can be found among the collection, but it is his pictures of the fonts at Luppitt and Toller Fratrum, that for me, stand out. Piper achieved his dramatic images in part by using a sponge to dampen the stone and enhance the depth of relief, and in doing so presented them as artworks of eldritch beauty. Some of these photos were included in an important article he wrote for the October 1936 edition of the *Architectural Review*. Here Piper argued forcefully for these sculptures to be taken seriously and aligned them with modernist experiments in form and composition. He wrote about the font at Toller Fratrum that 'it has the bigness and strangeness that has been accessory to so much of the achievement of Picasso, and through him and others to the aesthetic revelations of the twentieth century.' This font was a favourite of his. He visited several times in the 1930s, on one occasion driving through the night from his home in Henley just to show it to friend.

A few days later, I managed to get out to Toller Fratrum myself. Where the single-track road ended in mud there was the burnt shell of a manor house, largely hidden behind a web of scaffolding and plastic sheeting that squeaked and groaned like some kind of ailing creature. The day was an overcast one, the sounds eerie as they echoed around the abandoned yard that it fronted. Adjacent and serene was the church of St Basil, the path to it through the churchyard lit by late-flowering daffodils and offering a commanding view across soft, pale-green hills fringed with trees.

Inside, the font was right by the door and immediately impressive:

faces gazed out from the stone, hands raised to grip the cable-moulding that ran lazily around the top; a beast with two bodies and one head was propped upon columns; tiny heads peeped out of obscure angles. The whole ensemble was oddly inviting, a paradoxical combination of great energy and icy calmness, and somehow both ancient and modern at the same time. While many of the faces had been repaired, the power of the piece was undiminished. There was something mesmerising about these figures hanging on to each other in the silent church interior, and in my head Piper's magnificent phrase kept repeating: 'bigness and strangeness'.

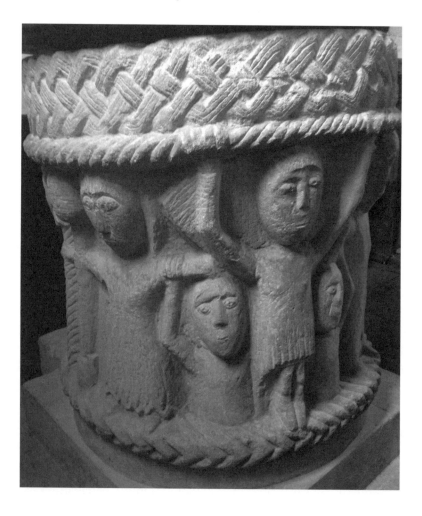

It wasn't until the later eleventh and early twelfth centuries that stone fonts became widely used. Earlier rites of baptism had taken place in a variety of settings, from the architectural (towers and porticos) to the natural (such as rivers). The production of stone fonts changed this flexibility of practice, however, locating the rite firmly within the church building. Baptism – the symbolic entry point to the Christian faith – now had a fixed receptacle for holy water. Within the small spaces of a Romanesque parish church, fonts were important, devotional objects that emphasised the life and death and life to come of the Christian soul. The stone of the font stood at the boundary of worlds. It mediated between the ordinary and the divine, and the imagery carved into it was like a bridge between the two.

I got up from inspecting the font and walked over to the altar to look at the fragment of Romanesque figure sculpture set into the wall. It's from a much larger piece of work depicting Mary Magdalene washing Christ's feet, but the tiny piece of it left, simply a head and a foot and a section of robe, carried such a moving presence that I felt sad thinking about the amount of work now lost. Piper was right to find in these works the hand of an artist. He recognised the quality and aspired towards a similar character in his own work. Writing about the font at Penmon, in Anglesey, he described it as having

> something about it that allowed the craftsman to work with the whole of *himself*, and at the same time to produce something that was above all lucid and popular: not in the least 'highbrow.' This is a capacity that the present-day artist envies, and strives for.

Few shared Piper's passion or his artistic insight. One of the problems was the overwhelming, and lingering, love that Victorian and Edwardian England had for the Gothic style, especially that of the thirteenth century known as Early English Gothic, in which the simple lines and restrained elegance of stiff-leaf foliage lent churches a nuanced, geometric perfection. The work of this period was 'pure, amazingly pure' according to the scholar Émile Mâle, whose *Religious Art in France of the Thirteenth Century* would set the tone for the era. And yet even he would succumb to the power of the Romanesque, writing a companion volume on the twelfth century a decade or so later, in 1922, questioning many of his earlier opinions. Such reflective prose, however, was the exception.

Piper was not completely alone in helping to turn the general perception of Romanesque sculpture around. In Devon in the early part of the twentieth century, the Romanesque fonts of the county found an ally in the form of the writer and historian Kate Marie Clarke. Clarke was born in Dulverton, Somerset, in December 1854, the second child to Isaac and Elizabeth. She had an elder sister, Margaret, and in time, three younger siblings: Edith, Frederick and Frank. Her father ran a drapery business which was a success, judging by the changes in address in the census returns: from 13 Market Place, Penzance, in 1861 to 2 Mont le Grand, Heavitree, Exeter from 1883 until the mid 1920s. The houses at this last address are classical buildings of two or three storeys, many with tremendous views over the suburbs to the hills beyond. Wherever she lived there were always domestic staff, servants, cooks, housemaids. Like her sisters, she never married.

Against this comfortable background Clarke came to writing relatively late in life, with her first work published in 1904 when she was fifty-one. This was her essay on the medieval priories of the city, published in an early edition of *Devon Notes and Queries* as 'The Conventual Houses of Exeter and the Neighbourhood'. For this she had been awarded the Gilchrist Medal, and its warm reception marked the start of an intensive two decades of research and publication on the medieval architecture and sculpture of Devon. Her contribution was a substantial one. She wrote not only the first significant work on the misericords of Exeter Cathedral but a series of nine articles on the Romanesque fonts of Devon, published between 1913 and 1922. Her work was often distinguished by a rare clarity, of both illustration (she was a skilled photographer) as well as mind. She was careful in taking the trouble to work out complex imagery and worked in collaboration with her friend and fellow historian – the spectacularly named Beatrix Feodora Clara Augusta Grace Cresswell (1862–1940) – to do so. Cresswell's line drawings of the carved fonts of the county allowed Clarke to see the sculpture clearly, and as a result, she avoided the mistakes introduced by other writers.*

Both Piper and Clarke wrote about numerous Romanesque fonts, but I tend to associate each with a particular example: Piper with Toller Fratrum and Clarke with Stoke Canon in Devon. As I started to think about leaving St Basil's and returned to the font to take some more photos, I wondered why this was the case. Piper had seen in the sculptured font at Toller Fratrum an artist with a wild eye, whose forms and figures had the power to bewitch the viewer several centuries after their creation. I had the impression that Clarke was similarly entranced by Stoke Canon. Certainly, it was a piece that she'd paid considerable time to, writing an article about it and two others – St Marychurch, near Torquay, and Alphington, in the Exeter suburbs, though she'd found the imagery 'very puzzling'. Her photograph in this article showed the font in partial darkness, marked out by its four corner figures, each one with upraised hands like the figure at Toller, holding the band of cable ornament that ran around the middle of the piece and that divided it from the circular bowl of the upper part. At first glance it would appear that these corner figures were wearing comically tall and thin hats, but on closer inspection these hats had rudimentary legs and tails that twisted across the stone. They were in fact lions, as Clarke identified, inverted ones, each one grasping the head of the human immediately below in their open jaws. A difficult situation to be in: hang on to the font, but do so with your head in the jaws of an upside-down man-eater.

A few days after my trip to Toller Fratrum I went to see the Stoke Canon font for myself, when visiting my friend Lynne in Exeter. We'd made the journey before, on a different day of the week, only to find the church locked, but I'd checked ahead this time and it looked like it would be open that Saturday morning. I hoped we'd be able to get in while people were setting up. In Lynne's dark-blue Nissan

---

* For example, the band of ornament around the bowl at Dean Prior, misidentified by Pevsner as 'two long distorted dragons' was, for Clarke, working from Cresswell's field sketches, clearly a band of 'conventional foliage', a description she later changed to 'a band of incised quasi-classical design'.

Micra we weaved along Alphington Road, heading out of the city. It was a cold morning but the sun was out. Stoke Canon lies on the low ground a few miles to the north of Exeter, and only a few winters back much of the surrounding land was under water. A double-decker was negotiating the long medieval bridge that led into the village. Squeezed into the side of the road we waited for it to pass, watching the driver gingerly ease it past an unfazed horse and apologetic rider. By ten o'clock we were there and the church was open.

Romanesque fonts in Devon churches are often remnants of a building long lost, one that has been replaced by a newer, bigger, more modern version. The font at Stoke Canon is no exception. Close up, it was even odder and more brutal than I'd previously understood. There were the cylindrical lions sinking their teeth into the heads of the human figures beneath. In between these poised human and beast pairs were other figures, not unlike those at Toller Fratrum, with oval heads and oval eyes, long tunics and pointed shoes, one holding a staff, another what looked like a book. There were interlaced crosses on the bowl and star motifs along the base.

Lions in Romanesque sculpture usually appear in a generic form: a quadruped beast with its tail curved up between the legs (much like the ones at Treneglos in Cornwall). Several examples can be found in Devon too, from the slender, foliate tailed pair on either side of a human figure on the tympanum at Down St Mary, to the hunched beasts on corbels at Sidbury or on the font at Topsham. Lions were ambivalent figures in medieval art and could be interpreted as both negative and positive, depending upon their setting. It was the wildness of the creature that informed both interpretations. Like the natural world this could be perceived as a threat to human society, something needing close control or conquest; yet at the same time such raw power might suggest a supernatural presence or divinity.

Lynne struck up a conversation with one of the people setting up for the event, a helpful distraction that allowed me to crawl around the back of the font and take some pictures. In any age this font would stand as a significant achievement, carved as it was from a single piece of the extremely hard, local volcanic stone, a pale purple colour and pitted with air bubbles from when it cooled as lava, millions of years ago. Even the shallow incised lines struck me as hard work, and the hollowing out of the bowl must have been unforgiving.

More people started to arrive in the church. Lynne finished her conversation and I had my photographs; we decided to leave before getting in the way. There were similarities between Stoke Canon and Toller Fratrum, I felt. It wasn't just the shared postures of the figures raising their hands and holding on to a decorative band, but something else, something much more intangible. That spot, in between two different states, movement and stillness, life and death, the Romanesque carvers found again and again. At Toller Fratrum the figures with their hands raised looked like they were holding up the bowl of the font itself. Were they supporting the font or being supported by it? Were they hanging on or praying? Were some being baptised? There were no simple answers.*

When John was back from his travels, and before I moved on from house-sitting, we made good on our plan to visit the churches at Luppitt and Dunkeswell. On a narrow road in hilly country, the early June green of hedges and freshly leaved trees broke now and again to give spectacular views across valleys bursting with vegetation. I hadn't checked ahead to make sure that either would be open, however, and as we walked through the graveyard at St Mary's in Luppitt I feared seeing the doors to the porch closed with a chain. But the chain was unlocked, the doors opened easily, and as we entered into the dark interior of the nave a gentle breeze carried a scent of roses from a nearby garden.

Pevsner hated this font, which stands beneath the west tower, and described it as 'the most barbaric "native" kind'. Carved in deep relief,

---

* Brunsdon Yapp suggests that the font at Toller Fratrum displays three distinct narratives: (1) Moses enabling the Israelites to defeat the Amalekites; (2) a conflation of the worship of the golden calf and the motif of two serpents attacking a man; and (3) a group of three figures, either Christ or St Michael saving souls from Hell. According to this interpretation the sculpture as a whole thereby represents triumph over evil and regeneration through Christ.

it is a compendium of everything that he disliked (and that Piper loved) about the Romanesque: asymmetrical, the images without boundaries, each face of the square bowl punctuated by a mask-like head on the corner. One of them was a Green Man, foliage tumbling from under a row of teeth (there was no lower jaw) to roll across one face of the font in succulent leaves, while on the other side they darted into the path of an amphisbaena – a dragon with an angry head at the end of its tail. There was a centaur holding a spear, two men hammering a giant nail into a disembodied head, a striated mask of a beast worn like a hat, and an animal being hunted by smaller ones that might be dogs. Eyes and teeth and heads pulsed with a strange energy.

The Devon historian W. G. Hoskins thought it was tenth century and Kate Clarke called it 'an undoubted Saxon font'. Today it is considered to be early Norman and a date of somewhere around 1100 wouldn't seem too far amiss. The Green Man on the corner of the bowl is replicated in similar fashion (no lower jaw, a strong line of teeth, sausage-like foliage) at the top of a fragment of column at the opposite end of the church.

The evening before our visit, as John was digging out broad beans from furry pods for the curry he was making, I tried to explain my project, in which he had become an unwitting participant. He listened to me struggle to explain my love for the peculiarities of Romanesque sculpture, from the simple geometric shapes repeated in dizzying combinations to the monsters and abstract figures, here and there jumping in to clarify or add something to my meandering thoughts. Knowing he had carved a few pieces in Romanesque style, I wondered what it was that he liked about the images?

'The ambiguity, there's something freeing about not knowing what it is exactly, what's going on.' Another bean pinged into the pan. 'It's sophisticated because it's ambiguous, which also means that it can be interpreted in all manner of ways – I think this is where the problems start,' he added.

'Everything gets narrowed down, you mean?'

'Yes, sort of, or rather in the quest to discover "what it meant" the whole thing gets lost and becomes a pale imitation of itself, stripped of all its power – as if that's the only way we can understand it.'

I knew what he was getting at. During my studies at Southampton I'd spent much of my time trying to understand the competing and often contrary interpretations of medieval architectural sculpture. Few writers came close to the art historian Michael Camille (1959–2002), whose insights enable us to understand the world in which the carvings were made as a complex, intelligent one. His book *Image on the Edge*, published in 1992, was largely responsible for reintroducing 'marginal' medieval images – from gargoyles to the doodles in manuscripts – as an area for academic research. His nuanced ability to understand images within the various contexts in which they'd been produced meant that he was acutely aware of the difficulties of drawing a neat conclusion. Our own cultural and personal experiences mean that, even if there was a definite meaning in the mind of the creator of the image or the patron who commissioned it, we would be unable to read it in exactly the same way as they would have. In many respects, as Camille suggested, 'multiple misinterpretations and partial comprehensions' were the best that we could achieve.

For much of the nineteenth and twentieth centuries, however, the interpretation that gained the most exposure was one born out of a romantic novel. This was Victor Hugo's *Notre-Dame de Paris*, published in 1831 and translated into English as *The Hunchback of Notre Dame*. In this his message was clear. 'In the Middle Ages men had no great thought that they did not write down in stone.' Medieval art, according to Hugo, was a universal system, the cathedrals and churches nothing more than sculpted and painted encyclopedias made for the sole purpose of educating the illiterate, who would be able to read them rather than books. This 'picture book' theory was supported by the influential art historian Émile Mâle, who, in 1898, published *The Gothic Image*, his monumental work on the art of thirteenth-century France. In the preface he set out his argument:

To the Middle Ages art was didactic. All that it was necessary that men should know – the history of the world from the creation, the dogmas of religion, the examples of the saints, the hierarchy of the virtues, the range of the sciences, arts and crafts – all these were taught them by the windows of the church or by the statues in the porch … Through the medium of art the highest conceptions of theologian and scholar penetrated to some extent the minds of even the humblest of the people.

How could it not be clearer? All medieval sculpture would have a 'key' to its unlocking somewhere, in a text or illustration from which it had been copied.

One of the problems with this theory was that it neutralised the power of images – they were secondary to texts and derived their meaning from them and them only. In this way, the lively visual world encountered throughout medieval architecture was reduced to one correct message that might be found with enough diligent searching of the archives. As researchers headed out to look at architectural sculpture it became apparent that not all examples might be so easy to understand. Images for which there was no 'written authority', where the meaning was unclear and where it was assumed that 'theological supervision was less strict', were generally taken to be the result of the 'individual fancies of the mason-carvers'. These, of course, were the very people assumed to be completely illiterate. Rather than pursuing this and investigating the worlds to which the carvers *did* have access too – sermons, stories, folktales – this formative period of sculpture studies assumed that a great deal of architectural carving was done by ignorant men, carving images they could neither understand nor explain. It seemed a wholly unsatisfactory answer.

Pity the Green Man, then, born during this period and shoehorned into a role as a pagan fertility figure more suited to the bohemian notions of the later twentieth-century counterculture than its medieval setting. Named as such in an article published in *Folklore* in 1939 by Julia Somerset, wife of eminent folklorist Lord Raglan, the name entered wider circulation through its use in Pevsner's *Buildings of England* series. Carved in stone and wood throughout medieval churches and cathedrals, the basic template is that of a face that sprouts leaves, which emerge from the mouth or nose or eyes, but there are numerous variations on this theme.

From the outset, however, the ability of the Green Man to lend itself to various, often conflicting, interpretations, suggested a longevity unrecognised in other medieval motifs. Somerset (or Lady Raglan, as she is credited in the article), noted the tendency of the carvings to defy categorisation, though she was firmly on the side of the Green Man being 'a man and not a spirit'. Within its medieval setting, the identification of the human body with the seasonal growth and decay of plants highlighted the impermanence of the physical world and our place within it, an idea given weight by its appearance on tomb slabs and other funereal sculpture. But the leaves might also represent breath, the gift of life first given to Adam and Eve in Eden. Sin and salvation, death and life: the Green Man remains an enigma, seemingly hovering in the metaphysical spaces between life and death. The Luppitt Green Men are early examples, though are not the oldest in Devon. The Saxon font at Dolton includes a head from whose nostrils two foliate-like dragons emerge – dragons being closely associated with the raw energy of nature in this period and not yet the universal symbol of evil they would later become.

The Luppitt font drew together a number of strong images, from depictions of force and violence (the hunting of an animal, the spike being hammered into a disembodied head), the monstrous (centaur, amphisbaena) to the quasi-mystical (Green Man). Beyond the fact that the rich carving suggested that the font was an object of status, the subject matter of the carvings placed it in a transitional zone as a vessel for holy water for the rite of baptism, marking the entry into the Christian life and all the dangers inherent in such a spiritual path. Monsters in medieval architectural art were often warnings, a way of drawing attention to spaces beyond the normal, where the divine and the human worlds overlapped. That such images could be carved on high-status items such as fonts also suggests that they were perceived in some way to be powerful themselves, perhaps with an apotropaic quality, and thereby able to magically protect the contents – and perhaps the users of those contents – from harm.

After leaving Luppitt, John and I drove a few miles further down the road to the church of St Nicholas, Dunkeswell. In the churchyard an ancient yew sheltered a carpet of strong-smelling wild garlic. It was hard to imagine on such a still morning that this village had been closely involved in global conflict, but the Second World War came closer here than it did to many other rural parishes of the county. In 1943 Dunkeswell Aerodrome was opened, initially for use by RAF Fighter Command and then RAF Coastal Command, but soon transferred to the United States Army Air Force 479th Antisubmarine Group. They based their specialised B-24 Liberator bombers here, flying missions over the Bay of Biscay. In November of the same year, the squadron was reassigned to the US Navy, which continued the antisubmarine missions out of Dunkeswell, their crews training with the RAF – the first US Navy unit to do so. Until November 1944, when the squadron moved to the airfield at Upottery further east, American heavy bombers were a familiar sight in the skies over this quiet corner of east Devon.

The American forces brought a touch of glamour to rural Devon: 'Miss Dunkeswell to be Crowned Tonight' runs the headline of a piece from the base's newspaper, *The U. S. Navy Liberator*, on July 1, 1944, a gala event for which the ten-piece Seabee Orchestra from the Exeter base were due to play. They also brought the horror of the war, too, with numerous sorties aborted, planes downed or damaged. The church at Dunkeswell paid a heavy price, with the Victorian tower destabilised by the vibrations of the B-24's engines to the extent that it became unsafe and had to be demolished in 1947 (a new one was built seven years later). The Romanesque font, though severely cracked and split by that point, remained undisturbed.

The historian W. G. Hoskins described the church at Dunkeswell, perhaps unfairly, as 'wholly uninteresting except for the primitive

Norman font, which has one of the earliest English representations of an Elephant'. The church, entirely rebuilt in 1868 by the architect C. F. Edwards of Axminster, looms in an austere Gothic; the elephant, a rare image to find in medieval sculpture of any date, is likely to be the earliest example in Britain.

The carving around the font is divided into eight panels by a series of arches and columns, each with simple capitals. In each panel the images are (as described by Christina Corser, Devon's compiler of material on Romanesque fonts), as follows:

1. A monk (?).
2. Bishop with crozier; right hand raised in benediction.
3. Man and woman.
4. Apparently part of a boat (see Clarke 1914).
5. Elephant. Is it attacking a dragon?
6. Archer shooting an arrow at an elephant.
7. Priest with cross.
8. A man with a spear and a shield.

There's something refreshing about Corser's unsettled and questioning notes: they suggest that this imagery resists description, that there is a mysterious quality to it still, that despite the damage there is something of substance still there. Dunkeswell had appealed to John Piper too, particularly regarding the 'man and woman' which he'd photographed twice. In the strong charcoal tones of his image they lean out of their background, each holding the other, eyes wide, faces open, their bodies split across the chest by a wandering crack. It's the most human carving of the eight, if not the most famous.

That accolade falls to the elephant. Is it attacking a dragon? It would appear so, trampling on the body of a snake-like creature with great pointed toes. In medieval art and thought the elephant was understood to reproduce infrequently and as such be a chaste animal. The source of the conflict between the dragon and the elephant was understood to lie in the peculiar qualities of each, the dragon possessing poison of great heat, the elephant having very cold blood. The dragon, wishing to cool itself, seeks the blood of an elephant in order to do so and devises numerous attempts to trap and kill the creature. The longstanding enmity between the two lent the elephant wholly positive associations in medieval Christian symbolism.

I sat down next to the font to take some pictures. With its uneven architectural lines and sea of faces it was hard not to see the font at Dunkeswell as a worn monument to a long-distant past, unapproachable and isolated within its rebuilt nineteenth- and twentieth-century church, like an animal that has lived too long. Here it had sat out the centuries, losing its form ever so slowly, prey to the fortunes of politics and wars and changes in religious thought. It wasn't easy to grasp something so alien, whose imagery appeared archaic and broken.

I didn't finish the mermaid I'd started in John's workshop. I had the shape and the decoration around it completed, though, which was a good start, and I could do the rest at another time. I wrapped it in bubblewrap and carried it on the bus to Poole Station, hoping the handles would hold and the material wouldn't split crossing a road or getting on the train.

There are many ingredients that psychologists identify as crucial to meaningful work. The one that strikes me the most as a stonecarver is a sense of connection. This is not only to the material and the place from which it comes, but to where I've carved it and the circumstances around its making. The piece of limestone I had carved was from the coast of Dorset – Portland – and its characteristics were specific to that place. Working it in Dorset added something to the process of making, a sense of anchorage, which it will hold for me once it is finished.

I thought of the font at Dunkeswell and imagined the carver setting to work, a world of images from which to draw. There were parallels with other carvings in the county. The presence of an archer leaning out of his frame to shoot an arrow at the awkward-looking elephant was a link with the font at Alphington, in Exeter, on which an archer shoots an arrow into the chest of a foliate-tailed dragon.

Was it possible to see these pieces of medieval sculpture less as dead pieces of a dead past, and more as points of connection and interaction with place, a record of an emotional connection? The making of a thing has its own narrative, carries its own stories. There is mystery in the process, a point where, through the repeated actions of mallet and chisel, the stone is carving you as much as you are carving it. Beyond the obvious physical change taking place to the stone there is something happening behind the chisel too. It is a journey of discovery, with the work itself the bridge between stone and heart. Failure, disillusionment and disconnection are as much a part of this process as satisfaction and delight, though they are usually the first to be forgotten. If it's easier to sweep the stones that didn't work and the time spent upon them into the shadows, it is the shadows that are the real anchor and the points of disillusion the strongest connection.

If carved stones were part of a long and ongoing dialogue with place, then perhaps 'place' wasn't a place after all. As the train carried me on to the South East I wondered whether it wasn't more an action or an inheritance than a specific location, something that lived in the attempt to do something well, to make something out of raw material. It struck me that in many respects the physical product was less important than the making, for it was in the making that the connection was formed. Ultimately, there might be a better and more specific word for this, though as I drifted into a light sleep and the train rattled on, I struggled to think of one.

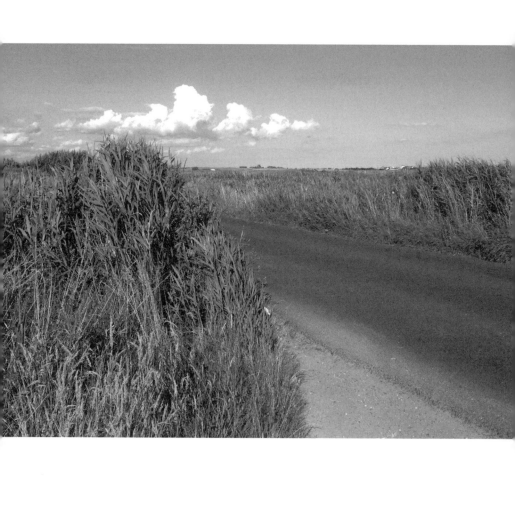

The Beasts of Bodmin

Out on the marshes the sun was blinding. There were no clouds and few trees, and what trees there were stood distant, stationed along the water-lined edges of broad fields. I'd come to see the deserted medieval village of Northeye, a once-thriving settlement on the Pevensey Levels in East Sussex, and had joined a group of about thirty people led by the curator of the local museum to visit the site. These days, the Levels are a closely managed resource, drained by ditches, the land rich with grasses for grazing cattle. They are also one of a handful of spots in the UK where the fen raft spider has made its home. A large and semi-aquatic species able to swim and hunt small fish, it lives in these peripheral waters that, as we walked, gently went about their business in forests of reed.

Despite growing up only couple of miles away, I'd never been out in the marshes to look for the original Northeye. The road and rail links speed past what looks, on the surface, like an empty landscape. The name has always intrigued me. Northeye. A small hill of Wadhurst clay peeping above the once waterlogged Levels. There are several 'eyes' or islands in this part of the world: Horse Eye (the island for horses), Manxeye (the monk's island), Langneye (the long island). Sometimes they are spelt without their final 'e' like Pevensey or Rickney. Each is only a few metres above sea level, and most are simply small areas of permanently dry land in the marsh that were once big enough for a few houses or livestock. Trace the contours on an Ordnance Survey map and it's possible to reconstruct the strange and unfamiliar medieval coastline, peppered with these small islands.

The water has left behind a legacy of secrets. HM Prison Northeye (1969–1992) was built on high ground a mile or so north-east of the medieval site on a former MoD radar station. When I was younger I imagined the marsh as a land of escaped prisoners and deadly stretches of water, a place where the real and the fantastic overlapped, a flashpoint where the undercurrents of the past threatened to surface.

We followed the marker posts, crossed multiple footbridges and bounced over thick grasses woven with yellow vetch until we reached the lower slopes of Chapel Field, a gentle hill topped with a feathery crown of nettles. Recorded as Nordeia in 1188 (and then Northye or Northie in 1264, Norzie in 1341 and Northey in 1724), the settlement was probably established as early as the eleventh century, its church perhaps one of the two in Bexhill mentioned in the Domesday Book. Its tiny chapel dedicated to St James was rebuilt in the thirteenth century and served by a priest until the sixteenth, after which it fell into ruin. In 1857 an artist recorded its last standing section of masonry, the drawing later engraved and published in the *Sussex Archaeological Collections*. This showed a sorry-looking fragment of architecture top-heavy with vegetation, 'the walls ... composed of flint boulders and very thin bricks', its rubble core exposed, a small window like an open wound. The stone was gradually robbed out and reused by locals. By the time the twentieth century rolled into view only the foundations remained. Northeye now is a ghost, a remnant, a shadow in the pasture, a flicker on the tongues of cattle.

Archaeologists have been drawn here twice to excavate the chapel. The first time was in 1938, the dig carried out by a local school under the direction of an enthusiastic teacher; the second was in the early 1950s. The first attempt ended abruptly with the outbreak of war, the second unpredictably, with the loss of most of the finds. One photograph from the Fifties shows the men in thick flannels and tank tops, hair slicked back, a plan or map open before them. In another, sections of carved architectural stones are stacked up beside the trench as they stoop to light a pipe or lean on a shovel. What happened to these fragments? Are they really, as some rumours suggest, beneath someone's driveway? The other finds? Even the archaeology has been bent to the will of the place, it seems, contributing more stories, more half-truths. In a transient landscape expect nothing solid, it seems to say. Fish-eating spiders seem a suitably topsy-turvy inhabitant here.

Post-medieval Northeye must have been a melancholy sight. Fragments of houses, drifting livestock, a crumbling chapel silhouetted

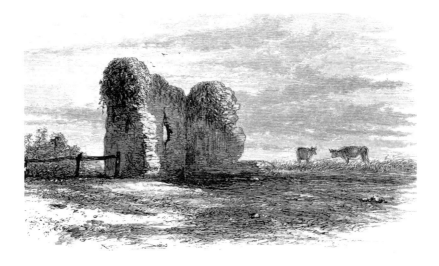

against the silver sea. In the deed of endowment of the chapel, drawn up in 1262 between John Clymping (the Bishop of Chichester) and William de Northeye, it is written that 'the said chapel be illuminated with three pounds of wax tapers annually on the Feast of St James' and that this 'be in force forever'. The feast of St James falls on July 25th, a few days after our excursion into the heat of the marshes. The lights went out over five hundred years ago, but I'm tempted to wonder if there was a vestige of them lighting this summer pilgrimage. We walked back past edgy cattle to a path fringed with head-height nettles and the welcome shade of trees. In the car park at its end, mirrors and windscreens and metal glittered with spikes of sun.

★

Here's a story of another Northeye, this one without the 'e': Neville
Northey Burnard (1818–1878). In the mid-1870s he closed his
London workshop for the last time and returned to Altarnun in
Cornwall, the village where he was born. The son of a stonemason,
he was a prodigiously talented and self-taught sculptor. His
earliest pieces – a portrait of the preacher John Wesley, and his
own grandparents' tombstone – were carved when he was fourteen.
He turned his talents into a successful career and throughout the
mid-nineteenth century his work, predominantly portrait busts
and commemorative monuments, was in high demand. But in his
mid-fifties he turned to alcohol, neglected his work and left his
wife. Shortly afterwards, two of his four children died from scarlet
fever. He took to the road and returned to east Cornwall, repaying
the kindness of a bed or barn for the night by drawing portraits or
writing poems. He died in Redruth Workhouse in 1878, a tragic
end to a life marked by extremes of success and despair.

Burnard, or Northey as I'm calling him, was a recent discovery. It
was the name that jumped out at me, only a couple of days after my
visit to the deserted village of Northeye. In Sussex I'd picked up a copy
of Charles Causley's *Collected Poems* from a secondhand bookshop
ahead of a long train journey. Browsing through it on the way back
to Cornwall, I discovered 'A Short Life of Nevil Northey Burnard', a
poem which identified Northey closely with the land of Cornwall, the
very bones of it – the rocks – and his capacity to shape them, which
in so doing shaped his own life. The tragedy of this 'torn tramp, rough
with talents' was not only his vagrancy and poverty-stricken end, but
that his work seems to have been lost to posterity, his skills overlooked.

I called in with Marcus in Falmouth the next day to see if he was
still on for the field trip we'd planned. He was, and as we later drove
up to the church of St Nonna at Altarnun I told him about my
recent visit to Northeye and my discovery of Northey, the strange
coincidence of finding out about him the day before hovering in the
back of my mind. Principally, the visit to Altarnun was to see the
font, one of the finest examples of Cornish sculpture from the late
Romanesque period. Now I would also be looking out for anything

related to Neville Northey Burnard.

The late Romanesque in Cornwall is interesting for a number of reasons, one of which is the appearance of 'mass-produced' fonts. The font at Altarnun is the best example of a group of ten nearly identical works that exist in the area. The design is a simple one: a square bowl supported by a central shaft carved with four heads, one on each corner, a rosette supported by a snake on the sides in between them. The snake is unusual for being a mirror image of itself, with no tail but another head, the two beak-like faces with protruding tongues turned to face each other.

In the middle of the county there was another group of fonts that replicated another design. These differed in almost every respect from the Altarnun group. There were fourteen examples; the best and most elaborately carved was at Bodmin. To help me visualise where they were, I'd made a map of Cornwall from photocopied sections of a road atlas glued into my notebook, onto which I'd stuck coloured dots, yellow for the Altarnun type and blue for Bodmin. Altarnun type fonts were all in east Cornwall and west Devon: Altarnun, Callington, Lanest, Lezant, Landrake, Launceston, Lawhitton, Jacobstow, Warbstow, Bratton Clovelly and Ashwater. The Bodmin type were found in churches generally in the middle of the county, between Truro and Bodmin: St Newlyn East, Roche, St Stephen-in-Brannel, Tregony, St Austell, Luxulyan, South Hill, St Kea, St Columb Minor, Mawgan-in-Pydar, St Wenn, St Ewe and Crantock. The two types of font, carved around the same time, were largely dependent upon different sources of stone: the blue elvan from Polyphant, near Launceston, for the former; the white elvan from around Pentewan for the latter, but this was not always the case. This probably explained much of their distribution too, the heavy pieces of stone travelling relatively short distances from the quarries and associated workshops.

Altarnun village sits in a hollow on the north-eastern edge of Bodmin Moor. There was a ford and a narrow bridge across the river, Penpont Water (a tributary of the River Inny), which joined the Tamar further east. We parked up near the church. It was a hot day but the interior of the church was cool and welcoming.

Group 1: Bodmin, St Newlyn East, Roche ①

Group 2: St Stephen-in-Brannel, Tregony ②

Group 3: St Austell, Luxulyan, Jarth Hill ③

Group 4: St Kea ④

Group 5: St Columb Minor, Mawgan-in-Pydar, St Wenn ⑤

Group 6: St Ewe, Crantock ⑥

~~Group 7~~: Tintagel, Cubert

opin/5

15

Kea closer to Group 2 than any others.

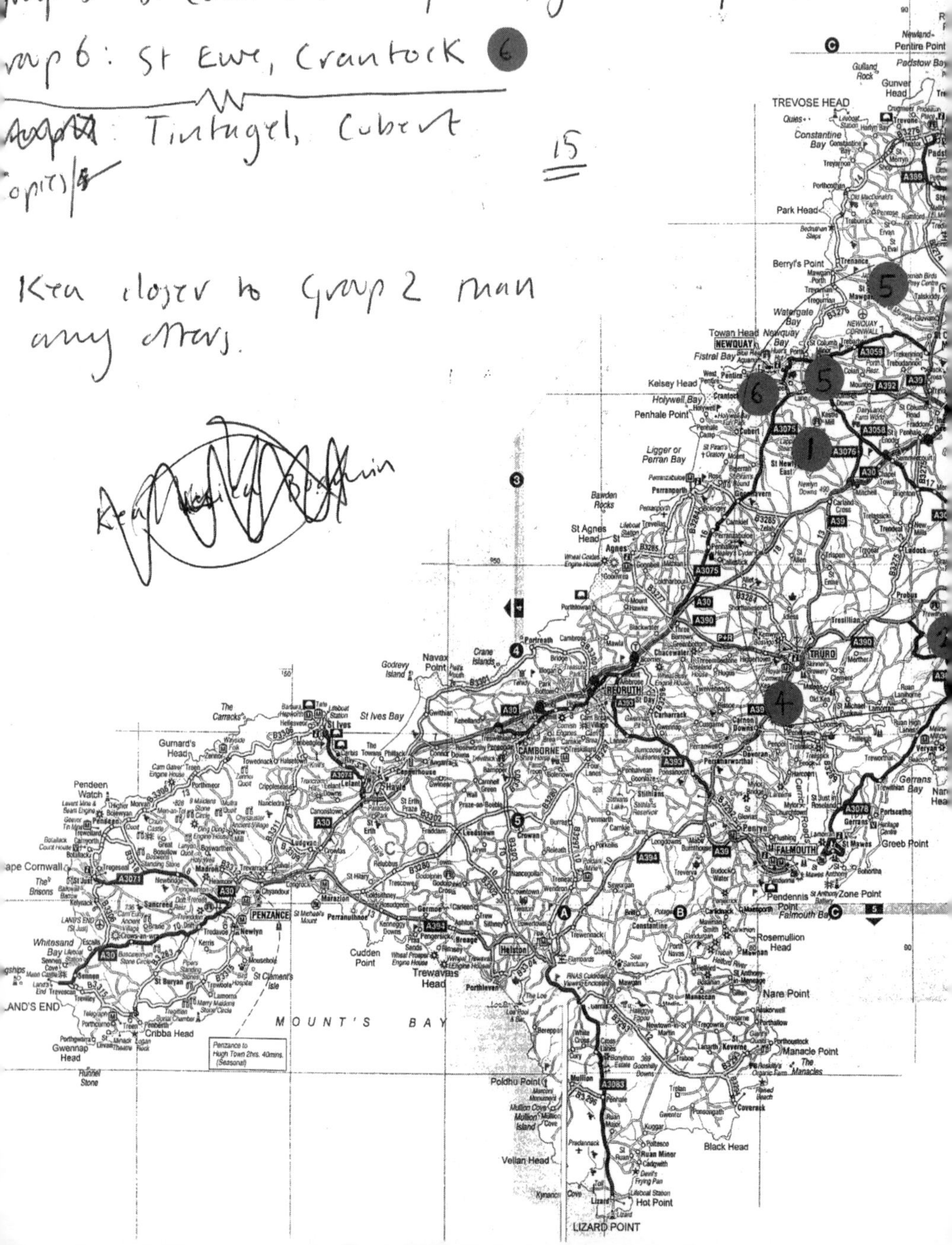

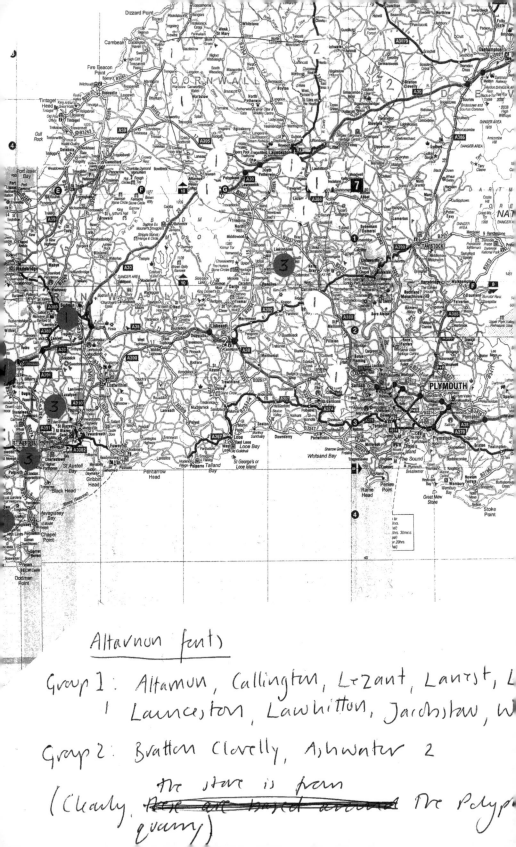

Altarnun fonts

Group I: Altarnun, Callington, Lezant, Lanrst, L
1 Launceston, Lawhitton, Jacobstow, W

Group 2: Bratton Clovelly, Ashwater 2

(Clearly, ~~these are based around~~ the store is from the Polyp
quarry)

Carvers speak of how Polyphant is delightful to work, soft and flecked with colours that sparkle when polished. The twentieth-century font in Chichester Cathedral by John Skelton, a nephew of Eric Gill, shows this well: the dark-green stone speckled with browns and pinks. At Altarnun the stone was in good condition, the faces clear, though there was a reddish tinge, perhaps traces of medieval paint. For the medieval carvers a good stone was one that could be worked, its natural finish unimportant once it was painted and gilded.

In 1901 Alfred C. Fryer published an article on this group of fonts. He was unaware of the two Devonian examples at Ashwater and Bratton Clovelly but wrote engagingly of the nine Cornish ones. He noted the 'strong family likeness', very late twelfth-century date and characteristic decoration, with 'each side adorned with a long-petalled flower, which is occasionally called the "Passion-flower pattern."' The 'stone employed in their construction, as well as their dimensions, varies considerably,' he goes on. On this last point he noted that the font at Jacobstow was formed from one block of granite, while Pentewan stone was used for the font at Laneast, and Polyphant for those at Launceston and Lawhitton. Looking at my map, I'd assumed that most, if not all, would be carved from Polyphant, the quarry located right in the heart of my pattern of yellow dots. Contrary to what I'd previously thought, this suggested that it was the design that took root here, upsetting the idea of a small workshop attached to a quarry churning out identical products in one type of stone.

The design was a flexible one, and, as Fryer noted, the 'heads at the four angles of the bowl are studies in themselves.' He contrasted the 'badly carved' ones at Landrake, Jacobstow and Warbstow with those he identified as well executed at Launceston and Altarnun, noting the remnants of paint at the latter, the faces flesh-coloured and the hair black. Two of the group differed from the standard heads-at-each-corner plan. At Lezant the corners of the font have been cut away, thereby removing all the heads and parts of the snakes and leaving only the large hexafoils intact. At Laneast one corner head was missing, replaced with a carving of a branch with seven leaves. The lower part of the bowl at Warbstow, and the west face of the bowl at Lawhitton, had been cut away too, losing the latter's geometric design. At Callington one face of the font appeared unfinished, the serpent and hexafoil replaced with an incised abstract design suggestive of a plant form.

As usual Sedding has some interesting things to say about the font at Callington, speculating both upon its method of manufacture as well as his own views of what might or might not be read into the imagery. 'The geometrical patterns in this case,' he suggests,

> are cut with fillets, instead of the usual sharp arris, on the raised lines of the patterns, thereby giving it a separate place among others of its kind. The fillets are about a quarter of an inch wide. The four heads at the corners may have had their origin in the four great writers of the Gospels, and the fact that these faces are often almost without expression and acutely hideous, does not disprove the theory. Indeed, most mediaeval imagery was wrought by simple-minded men, endeavouring by their art to portray those great symbolical figures which were worthy of expression in stone. The dragons, representing evil, appear to be in captivity. It cannot be correctly assumed, however, that this is a true reading of the sculptor's mind.

Sedding was clearly aware of the theories of interpretation in vogue at the time, and his addition of a caveat, that it cannot be assumed that this is what was in 'the sculptor's mind' marks him out as unusual, even if those men were 'simple-minded'. The sculptor's mind was generally ignored. Even thirty years later the author Mary Desiree Anderson could write without controversy that 'the carvers did not fully understand the symbolism of the subjects they represented', citing as evidence the 'countless inaccurate versions of beasts and legends to be found in parish churches throughout the country,' which were, for her, the 'attempts of illiterate carvers to reproduce the designs seen in the mason's lodge attached to some great cathedral, where they had been temporarily employed.'

Outside in the churchyard, I found the gravestone carved by Northey when he was fourteen to commemorate his grandparents – an easy find in comparison to the trouble of locating Sedding's gravestone at Crantock. It was a piece of slate, rectangular with small cusped leaves in the top corners and strong lettering. A piece of work to which any stonemason would aspire, but to think he completed it in his early teens was astonishing. Some of us, at least, get going early.

Back in my flat in Falmouth a few days later, I discovered a photograph of the font at St Cuby, Tregony, taken by John Piper (and mislabelled as St Stephen-in-Brannel) in the online Tate archive. It was a black-and-white closeup of one face carved with wandering geometric motifs and a small creature with a looping tail. A ghostly hand, possibly that of Piper's wife Myfanwy, appeared on one side of the image, holding up a piece of dark cloth to block out the light from the window behind. There was something in the asymmetrical layout and non-traditional spacing of the motifs that really worked, the mixture of designs and their simple execution capturing something peripheral and primal.

Tregony is one of several fonts known as the 'Bodmin type' after the exalted example in the church there. The Bodmin fonts rely on a handful of motifs and a coherent design: a large bowl supported on a central pedestal and four corner columns, the top of each terminating in a head. At Bodmin, St Newlyn East and Roche (perhaps the best of this group), these heads have angelic wings extending behind them onto the bowl itself. At other sites the wings are absent and only the heads, sometimes of the simplest design, stare out from the stone. The decoration, too, varies, from the flamboyant and deeply undercut foliage at Bodmin to none at all at St Ewe. St Erme is a good example of this group of carvings too, and even though it omits the corner columns and heads it retains the style of foliage, with stands of leaves on each side of the bowl and a running motif along the top.

The example at Bodmin has received high praise and deservedly so, the workshop responsible for its production ranked as one of the most outstanding for the period by George Zarnecki. If the phrase 'Into Bodmin and out of the world' alludes to the town's 'sleepy aspect' and the fact that it is cut off, it was not true in the early 1200s. It might seem strange now that this late flowering of Romanesque sculpture should take place here, in a town where the church is routinely closed throughout the winter months. But on the cusp of the Gothic, Bodmin was host to an outstanding stonemasonry workshop, and this was likely connected to the Priory.

Bodmin Priory grew out of an earlier monastic foundation dedicated to St Petroc that had been present on the site since the tenth century. It was the wealthiest of the Cornish minsters that survived the Norman Conquest, with the largest landed endowment of any minster at this time – much greater than Launceston, the next in size. It was re-established as an Augustinian priory in 1123–24 by the Bishop of Exeter. After this reorganisation the canons moved to a new location on the opposite side of the road, their old minster church being converted into the parish church for the town and, in the later medieval period, almost entirely rebuilt. (The only remaining trace of the minster is the tower attached to the north side of the nave.) The new twelfth-century priory must have looked fairly spectacular. The photographs of carved capitals included in Sedding's book (many of which were hollowed out to be used as planters in the vicarage garden) were of a late Romanesque style with repeating small arches interspersed with large beads and bulbous, abstract foliage that anticipated the drooping stiff-leaf style of the early Gothic. One of them has survived as a piscina in the church at nearby Lanivet. They are substantial pieces of work and suggested that the priory featured an imposing arcade of columns, whether dividing aisles from the nave or choir it is now impossible to tell.

There is another piece of evidence that adds to the limited remains of the Romanesque priory. This is a drawing of the original west door, long since replaced, described by Sedding as 'recessed with semi-circular arches, zigzag and other mouldings', each jamb containing 'two semi-detached shafts with carved capitals'. This drawing, probably dating to the eighteenth century, was copied and included in Sir John Maclean's three-volume history of Trigg Minor published in 1873. In the rigid style peculiar to some of the engravings of the period, the drawing shows a doorway of three orders, each one carved with chevron, the inner one also featuring interspersed beads or bosses. The capitals are carved with chevron, too, while a moulding of circular small bosses runs around the outside of the arch as well as horizontally through the masonry. There is no doubt that this rich, if slightly unimaginative, carving represents a high-status doorway, reminiscent of those at Kilkhampton, Morwenstow and St Germans.

The font, though, is the jewel of this late-twelfth-century workshop, one of 'the most interesting examples of Norman art to be found in the British Isles,' according to Sedding. He dated it, according to the

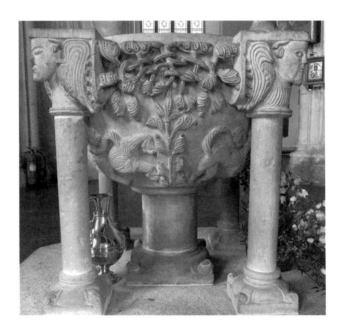

way 'in which the interlaced ornamentation is carved and under-cut' to the 'close of the Norman period, or during that described as the "Transitional" to "Early English," namely, circa 1190,' before turning to describe it:

Almost the entire external surface of the bowl is enriched with vigorous and effective emblematic carving. The south side and the west are ornamented with flowers, the stems being twisted and interlaced in the customary Celtic manner. The two other sides are treated in a similar way, but represent serpents with their bodies knotted and twisted.

The evil-looking reptiles at the base of the bowl are symbolical of the evil spirits cast out at the Sacrament of Baptism, and the angel heads previously mentioned may represent the four archangels.

Sedding's 'evil-looking reptiles' are in fact lions, albeit highly stylised ones, the design another variation on the tree of life with accompanying beasts that we find, earlier in the century, at Treneglos. They have grinning faces and striated bodies, and tails ending in curling leaves. The wavering plant in between them sprouts regular abstract leaves and perhaps a central flower or bud of some kind, but this is overshadowed by the complex intertwinings of the foliage above them. The angel heads on each corner have wide, almond-shaped eyes and a decorative strip of beading contoured around the outer edge of their wings, an unusual detail but one that links it with the doorway and the remnants of capitals, all of which utilised, if not emphasised, the motif.

Sometimes the light in Cornwall is like powdered chalk in sea water, a tenebrous, glassy whiteness not unlike the colour of the waves that trouble the foot of the South Downs hundreds of miles to the east. Sometimes it's more like a torch shone through a slice of alabaster, translucent and dreamlike, slightly darker where it meets the land as if tainted by gravity and the proximity of the earth. At other times there is a quality found in old photographs or at the edges of a long-forgotten and faded tapestry, a grain or a texture. Under the leaves of the shimmering palms that framed the path to the porch at All Saints, St Ewe, I tried to take a picture that would somehow hold all this: the foliage lit up like stained glass in the diffuse light, the tower hazy in a gentle thermal. In places like this on such summer days, everything can seem slightly unreal, the subtropical plants and Gothic masonry making an unearthly paradise for both the living and the dead.

The door to the porch was open and beckoned me inside with the prospect of coolness. There were pamphlets for sale on the side, some secondhand novels on a revolving stand, and a tray of knitted 'baby's first boots' for £2 a pair, all proceeds to the church funds. There were some beautiful monuments on the wall, pale-coloured marble and fat voluted capitals adding an agreeable touch of the local to the classical style, making it a little less formal and more approachable.

Just as a fragment of sculpture can reveal much about the larger piece from which it originally came, so a single arch in a church might hold the invisible footprint of a feature long since lost. This is the case in the church at St Ewe, where one arch in the south arcade appeared to be larger than any other. This caught my attention, particularly as it stood opposite the north transept on the other side of the nave.

Romanesque churches generally consisted of a two-celled nave and chancel, sometimes with a tower, gradually expanded throughout the later medieval period with the addition of transept chapels and aisles, as changes in liturgy and society impacted upon the needs of the building. The building of an aisle often meant accommodating obstacles, and so the width of a pre-existing transept chapel could be preserved, as it was at St Ewe, in the irregular spacing of columns. The transept is no more, removed when the aisle was built, but its absent form lives on as a ghost in the arcade, the wide arch its only echo.

The font at St Ewe was one of the most basic of the Bodmin group, similar to that at Crantock, the characteristic decoration stripped back to the bare essentials of form. The heads at the top of the four corner shafts were the only decorative touches other than four stylised leaves at the foot of the main pedestal. While it was carved in the same type of stone as that at Bodmin, it was hard to imagine it as the work of the same carver. With its fleshy, luxuriant foliage and intricate carving, the Bodmin font provided a strong contrast to St Ewe's, where only the simplest template of that style was preserved (though, to be fair, carving a bowl of this size is impressive).

Back outside, the heat of the day hit me as I closed the door. Time seemed to have stretched inside the church, for there was plenty of afternoon left, which made my itinerary of St Kea, St Stephen, St

Newlyn East and Tregony still possible. I was interested in seeing some of the less known pieces of the Bodmin-style group – and in particular Tregony, where the Pipers were drawn. Once again, I was following in their footsteps, tracing multiple pasts.

At St Kea they were busy setting up for a service. This was the new church, crisp Victorian Gothic throughout, not the old one with the abandoned tower and the early Christian inscribed stone a mile or so up the road. The font stood beneath the tower at the west end, the design more intricate than the St Ewe example but still more abstract than that at Bodmin, each side bearing only one image. There was a lion-like beast waving its tail above its head on one side, striated foliage designs on two others, and a circular cross on the remaining face. The corner heads appeared serene, grooved lines on their necks perhaps meant to suggest the presence of wings, though these were absent on the stone behind.

It was half past three by the time I got to St Stephens. The sun was catching the top of the tower and there was a healthy-looking cutting of the Glastonbury thorn beside the path to the entrance. The grille on the outer doors of the porch was locked. Undeterred, I continued on to St Newlyn East. Here the font had been restored, the polished deep green serpentine columns added in 1883 providing a strong contrast to the pale elvan of the bowl. One of the four corner heads had been replaced but like that at Roche, the new carving was a good one and sensitively done. It was close in style to the Bodmin font though there were crucial differences. The foliage was less distinct, less undercut and less detailed. The beasts that gambolled around the base of the bowl were most likely lions, like those at Bodmin or the Treneglos tympanum from earlier in the century. The wings of the angel heads curled and disappeared into the swirls of foliage.

Tregony was closed by the time I'd arrived. Piper's image would have to do for now. As I headed back to Falmouth, I wondered about the Cornishness of fonts in the Altarnun and the Bodmin style. There was something very distinct about their shapes and replicated designs that echoed, to some extent, earlier medieval traditions of wheel-headed crosses in the landscape (the large, and centrally placed rosette motifs, for example). Then there was the use of local stones, Polyphant and Pentewan, a blue and a white elvan respectively, that now, in their unpainted state, lent subtle colours to their church interiors. But, in a sense, carved stones will always reflect the places from which the stone has come, anchoring us to these landscapes. They are points in time, and through time, that allow us to sense the past and allow it to seep into the present. In turn, they, like the medieval churches where they are found, become part of the landscape themselves, weathering back into it, taking the secrets of the centuries with them.

The particularities of these stones and their repeated motifs reminded me of something I'd read recently by the sculptor Barbara Hepworth, herself a settler in Cornwall and admirer of its landscape, who established her studio in St Ives after the war. 'Carving to me is more interesting than modelling,' she wrote,

> because there is an unlimited variety of materials from which to draw inspiration. Each material demands a particular treatment and there are an infinite number of subjects in life each to be re-created in a particular material. In fact, it would be possible to carve the same subject in a different stone each time, throughout life, without a repetition of form.

It seemed to me that this was exactly what these fonts illustrated: the same design repeated again and again was, each time, a new carving with its own sense of atmosphere and life. That such a restricted set of motifs could be so flexible and able to conjure up such different moods and feelings was incredible. But then I also remembered that we were introduced to this idea early on at Weymouth, when we had to carve a frieze with a repeating pattern.

Our tutor Chris had settled on a flower-and-leaf design, the flower to be of any shape so long as it had five petals. We were to carve a section each so that when the stones were placed together it would form a coherent run. I still have the maquette. We made it in clay first, then cast it in plaster, using plaster for the mould as well. This made its removal (the plaster mould from the plaster cast it contained, the two separated by a red slip and some grease) a task of intense concentration, some of us managing to break the mould into large sections while others went for a more considered approach with a small chisel. Most came out in one piece. With our models to hand for reference, we could then start translating the design into the soft Maltese limestone earmarked for the purpose, roughing out the waste, the areas of stone that would not feature as part of the design, and leaving 'blocked out' pieces to return to later for the more detailed carving. It was the first piece of work in stone many of us had done, and despite Chris's protestations against free carving, the exercise, even with a model to copy, allowed considerable creative freedom.

We took pictures of the completed pieces in the rainy yard at the back of the workshop, the grey sky and close-to camera angles instilling a sense of monumentality into our simple efforts. The designs were not complicated, and in fact, in the fixed layout of a five-petalled flower on one side and a scrolling stem with leaves on the other, they were identical. But we had each brought different leaves or flowers to the work, which lent the stones, placed side by side to form a frieze, a sense of life. It brought home just how visible the individual hand of the craftsman or craftswoman was, if you only looked closely enough.

Years later, as a stonemason, climbing the stairs of the north tower at Exeter Cathedral for the umpteenth time, I would remember this. Sometimes I imagined I could hear the laughter of the medieval masons. This was because about two-thirds of the way up, the depth of each step increased. There's no particular reason for it to do so, no obvious break in building phases, for example, that might suggest why. Just when your legs and lungs have had enough the masonry steps force you to reach higher, work harder. Out of breath, I cursed my twelfth-century predecessors who carefully folded these twisting steps into the thickness of the wall. They may be silent in the historical record, their personalities absent, their names lost, and their lives, on the whole, anonymous and invisible: but they were not silent here.

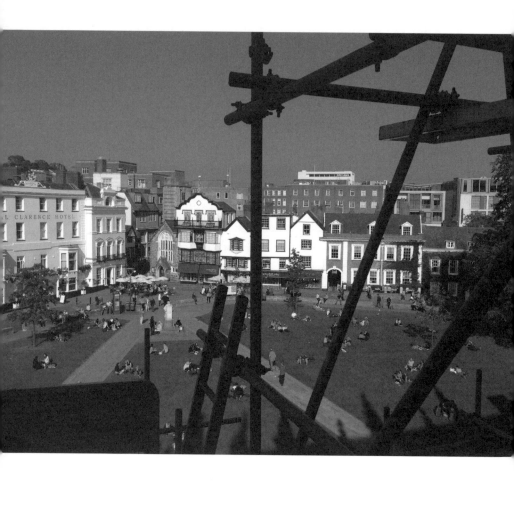

Cathedral Stonemason

A Wednesday morning in September and the sun was blinding as I walked through Falmouth to Prince of Wales Pier. I was off to catch the ferry across the Fal estuary to St Mawes, then pick up another, smaller, one that would take me across the Percuil River to Place. The point of the trip was to visit the church of St Anthony in Roseland, famous for its richly decorated Romanesque doorway. There was a light breeze, enough to carry a scent of the sea, but for the most part it was a still day. Arriving at my destination earlier than I'd imagined, I took a seat on a bench and studied the water for waves, slightly anxious that I hadn't been on a boat for some time. It was a consistent deep blue, darkening slightly further out from the town.

In my rush to leave the flat about fifteen minutes earlier I'd accidentally knocked some books off a shelf near the door. The one that fell onto the floor ejected a black-and-white postcard and some other papers that had been tucked into it and forgotten. I picked them up and put them in my bag, wanting to have a closer look when I got the chance. Waiting on the pier for the ferry, I reached into my bag and found the postcard. I'd bought it from the shop on Exeter quayside that sold secondhand books and curios, a regular Sunday afternoon haunt. It showed the face of the cathedral in sepia tones, probably sometime in the 1920s or 30s, the blackened stone a sombre backdrop to one or two elegant cars. At the southern end of the image screen there was a ramshackle piece of scaffolding, a spider of poles and planks half concealed by corrugated iron that offered an exposed working platform. Postcards rarely feature scaffolding, so this intrigued me: it was evidence of repair work and working conditions, things that are often overlooked in the grand narrative of cathedrals. The day-to-day work is where the real life of a building is found. The sculptor Mark Batten wrote of the connection that working stone established with your predecessors, how placing a new stone next to an old one created a link between the two masons, no matter how many centuries between them. But there was something else, something about the fragile platform that suggested that the work itself – and the masons carrying it out – were ephemeral compared to the building. This was just one more event in the long life of the west front, another repair.

As the ferry left the pier my anxieties dissolved. It was lovely out on the water. I should do this more often, I thought. The warmth and movement and smooth feel of the air seemed to relax all the passengers; people started speaking to each other; a pet dog that had been sitting upright lay down and closed its eyes. Crossing the stretch of water called the Carrick Roads, the boat started to rock a bit more but nobody seemed particularly bothered, lulled as we were by the rhythms of the glittering blue all around us.

At St Mawes we climbed the steps up from the ferry to the harbour wall. The air was soft and the land just across the river tantalisingly close. Leaning on a wall and waiting for the next ferry, I realised just how many worked granite blocks there were here, huge pieces of stone forming the harbour walls and slipway. The amount of work in these stones was impressive, as was the effort to get them here: no doubt the blocks were brought in by boat from the quarries in the country around Falmouth. The rivers and the sea have always been crucial means of moving stone, and historically many quarries have been cliffs, the stone extracted and immediately loaded into barges.

The sea has carried other, less benevolent, cargoes to the south coast. The Black Death entered England via a ship landing at Melcombe Regis (today's Weymouth) in June 1348, quickly working its way west through Devon and Cornwall and east towards London in the following months. The cataclysmic effects of the plague are well known; the swellings in armpit and groin that led to a swift, painful death; the reduction of the population by at least a third, leading to, for those lucky enough to survive, profound social and economic change. At Exeter its arrival coincided with the closing stages of the Gothic programme of rebuilding the cathedral. This had begun in the last quarter of the thirteenth century with the east-end chapels and gradually progressed west, dismantling the Romanesque architecture and rebuilding it in the Decorated Gothic style of the period. By the 1340s, work had reached the west front, and in 1342 the image screen – the tiers of stone angels, saints and kings that greets the visitor – was begun under master mason William Joy. Initially this was just two tiers but in the late fifteenth century it became three, its new height obscuring the base of the great west window. William Joy disappears from the records in the late 1340s and it is possible that he was a victim of the plague. If he was, then his last job – the carving and building of the image screen – became one of my first as a working stonemason, repairing it.

The interview to get the job included a practical test. In the carpenter's workshop, the air heavy with the smell of gloss paint, I picked up my tools and started.

'Are you really making notes?' I asked Gary, the head stonemason, who was standing nearby with a notebook.

'You're doing fine. Just keep going.'

'But you're writing notes about this, aren't you?'

'No I'm timing you. You've had five minutes already.'

'Am I at the right interview? I came for the stonemasonry and maintenance job.'

'Six minutes.'

'Okay.'

With a spanner I tightened the nut on the bolt I'd just put in.

'But...'

'Just put the bench together. At least we can sit on something.'

I'd received a phone call from Gary at the end of January. There might be a job coming up, he'd said – someone was leaving.

It was the best news I could have imagined.

A few months earlier I'd finished my course at Weymouth and had returned to Devon. I'd found a temporary job in an office doing data entry, typing in numbers from privately conducted surveys about healthcare from eight in the morning until four in the afternoon. Occasionally there'd be a comment; that would have to go in too. I lived for the comments, even the most mundane ones, anything to break up the incessant numbers. It was a mind-numbing job and it seemed like there was no way out. I made a decent friend, though. Brett hated the job too, often starting the day by cracking open a six-pack of cheap energy drinks which he'd proceed to work his way through as the day wore on. We'd try to get out in the fresh air as often as possible, volunteering for whatever jobs involved walking to other parts of the site, but despite our best efforts the work was crippling. Headaches spread like wildfires from my neck, up and over the top of my skull to my forehead and eyes, often lasting for days.

After work I'd walk back to the bus station via the cathedral, stopping to admire the west front. I'd knocked on the door to the mason's yard a couple of times asking for work, a strategy that had paid off. Three months later it was official: there was an advert in the local paper. Best of all, I'd got an interview.

By this point I'd done a fair bit of carving and was able to include photographs of several projects with my application. The best was from the end of the academic year at Weymouth, when there'd been a competition to carve a roof boss. This was a chance for the frustrated artisans among us to do a bit of free carving, the very thing that we'd been told at the start that we wouldn't be doing. We were each given a cube of Bath stone for the task and in preparation for the event made a maquette in clay to copy. We had three days to produce a fully carved piece that would be judged and prizes awarded.

Here I first saw everyone's unique hand. Knowing my fellow students as I did by then, this was more a confirmation of personality rather than a surprise. John (who won) carved a monkey on a mobile phone, its face contorted, a kind of simian Dom Joly; Wally had done the head of Darth Vader, perhaps the oddest thing I've seen carved in stone. Some looked effortless, as if they'd grown naturally; others were a bit more awkward, mine included. I'd carved a mermaid but hadn't bargained for a blank space right in the centre of the boss so I filled it with foliage – a technique beloved of my medieval ancestors – but it looked like the afterthought it was, especially as I carried a tendril of the unspecified plant around the edge of the boss itself. 'Good design is one hundred per cent of the job,' Chris had said to us one afternoon, and in the practice of carrying out my first free carving I'd begun to see just how true his words were.

The practical training at Weymouth, measurable in the sense of being able to produce, more or less, what was asked of us, had begun to encourage an unquantifiable feel for the material. We had become novice readers of stone, starting to work from experiences that gradually became instinct. An instinct that told us to leave a particular stone and select another, though sometimes this could border on superstition, a 'feeling in the bones'. Reading the stone for vents or flaws or shells became an art, and as I gradually found myself mulling over pieces of stone I realised that novice as I was, I too was developing this knowledge.

But the bench had thrown me. Was it a trick? As I put it together I wondered at what might be my new surroundings. The stonemason's yard occupied an awkward gap created by the east end of the chapter house, the south-east end of the cathedral and the west wing of the Bishop's Palace. Numerous workshops and buildings were clustered around the edges of this space: the mason's workshop itself, its blue doors flanked by the dust extraction unit and a small corrugated tin-roofed shelter to keep the weather off newly worked stones; the rest room or tea room for the masons; an office space; a door that led to a corridor where there were toilets and steps up to the cathedral shop; and the lead store, home to large pieces of machinery such as the scissor lift, though some remnants of lead remained.

Between the edge of the lead store and the corner of the scaffold rack was the first bit of accessible cathedral, the Chapel of St James. A Gothic door and steps down into a crypt-like space, complete with vaulting, led to the engineering for the organ. This was postwar

Gothic, the chapel entirely destroyed by the Luftwaffe in May 1942 along with a substantial part of the cathedral. There is a famous photograph of the damage in which the south nave aisle appeared as a cavernous maw open to the sky, the darkness of the interior contrasting with the white, broken arcades and the two flying buttresses above that had been sliced clean through. To the right, past this pinch point, the yard opened out again and there was another workshop (the carpenter's) beneath the passageway that led from the Bishop's Palace to the cathedral itself.

Putting together the flat-pack bench was one part of a three-part interview which also included undertaking some mortar repairs to Wiliam Joy's image screen on the west front of the cathedral and a formal discussion. There was one other candidate. Gary, however, was on my side. Amused as he was by my greenness as a stonemason he must have seen something, a spark of potential, something that nobody else did. I learned later that the panel had wanted to offer the job to the other applicant but he had intervened, persuading them to offer it to me instead. I was in.

The pontoon at Place wobbled as I stepped out of the ferry and walked carefully towards the concrete steps built into the rocks. The path led into a small area of trees before turning and following the edge of a field, then onto a road where there was a signpost to the church.

St Anthony in Roseland is connected to the history of the priory at Plympton in Devon, refounded by Bishop William Warelwast in 1121. William's successor (and nephew), Bishop Robert, gave to Plympton two of the Roseland churches, St Anthony and St Just, a grant later confirmed by Henry II. Shortly afterwards the priory of St Anthony was re-established according to the Augustinian rule (anywhere between 1138, the earliest possible year of Bishop Robert's grant, and 1231, when the priory was certainly in existence). The site had been that of a church or a chapel since at least the twelfth century.

The building stood in a small clearing, dappled by sunlight filtering through the leaves, the sharp green of summer vegetation a strong contrast with the cream-coloured stone of the doorway. It was an unusual door, not so much for the chevron ornament but for the way in which the inner orders of the arch worked together. The middle one was cusped so that it formed semicircles, each providing a frame around nine decorative segments on the inner order. Most were carved with stylised leaves, tendrils of plants, delicate and decorative foliage, each one different to its neighbour. Only one was carved with a geometric design – interlaced blind arcading, a motif firmly established among the Romanesque sculpture of north Devon and north Cornwall, appearing, for example, at Morwenstow, Parkham, Bondleigh, Shebbear, Buckland Brewer and Woolsery. Adding an asymmetrical twist was a small image of the Agnus Dei, contained within a circle on the otherwise uncarved stones of the innermost arch.

The stone of the doorway was not native to Cornwall. A buff-coloured limestone that weathered to pale grey, it was fine-grained and of good quality. It looked like Caen stone from Normandy and I later read that it was. If the carving hadn't already suggested high status and wealthy patronage then this – one of the best limestones available to medieval masons – certainly did. The presence of this high-quality carving on a French stone at a remote church has fuelled speculation that the doorway was an import, brought from the Augustian mother-house at Plympton, the idea being that it was a castoff and no longer needed when Plympton was being rebuilt. But I wasn't entirely convinced. From my work at the cathedral I knew that until a stone was fixed in place it could be a cumbersome object, difficult to manoeuvre and prone to damage. Romanesque stones that have been moved, such as the chancel arch at Creech in Dorset, now in a nearby Italianate chapel, often weren't in the best condition. Those at St Anthony in Roseland appear to have lasted the centuries relatively well. I imagine it's more likely that the doorway was a remnant from when the church was rebuilt or adapted during the twelfth century.

Sitting on the rocks in the sun, waiting for the ferry to take me back to St Mawes, I tried to recall the other Romanesque doorways in south Cornwall. Along with St Anthony in Roseland there were those at Landewednack, Cury, Mylor, Perranaworthal, St Michael Caerhayes, Looe and Rame. Some of these were fragments only. At both Perranaworthal and Rame, only the carved tympana, now reset, had survived, both discovered during renovation works undertaken during the 1880s. The one at Rame was carved with three circles, two of which contained crosses, the other a six-spoked star or rosette design. Its condition was, as Arthur Langdon observed in the early twentieth century, 'somewhat mutilated', having been used as a building stone. The doorway at Perranaworthal had fared better. Its main feature, an Agnus Dei, was bordered by a band of wavy foliage similar in style to that on the font at St Mary Steps in Exeter. The work showed close similarities with that at St Michael Caerhayes; perhaps both were accomplished by the same mason. The stones suggested that in the twelfth century the county wasn't as cut off or behind as it might have once been thought.

With Plympton Priory re-established in the early twelfth century by a Bishop of Exeter, links between it and the cathedral are likely. In a short article for the *Devon and Cornwall Notes and Queries* in 1920, Kate Clarke published a photograph of three carved corbels that had been discovered when an old cottage in Plympton was demolished. Likely to be relics of the twelfth-century priory, the stones had been reused as building material, the carved sides protected by being faced into the wall. Each one bore faces familiar to me from the north and south towers at Exeter, each neither wholly human or animal, with their almond-shaped eyes, querulous mouths and geometric noses. To some degree the choice of bold images would have been dictated by the stone, a coarse sandstone from Salcombe Regis on the coast of East Devon, the quality of which varied. But whatever stone they're carved in, the ambiguity of the carved Romanesque heads add a powerful presence to a building.

One of the things that had initially drawn me to medieval sculpture was its otherworldly quality. Much of it, especially the architectural work, seemed to be carved with creatures: dragons, mermaids, beasts with one head and two bodies, things that were both human and animal. If you spent a lot of time looking at medieval sculpture, the monstrous became normal; there were chimeras everywhere.

My doctoral research had also been an exploration of the grotesque, a word that is as difficult to pin down as its subject matter. It was invented to describe a particular feature of first-century Roman wall painting that had been discovered through the excavation of ruined villas and bathhouses in fifteenth-century Italy. The images that struck a chord were not the centrepiece of each wall painting, mural or fresco but rather appeared as a frame or border surrounding empty spaces, landscapes, or mythical scenes. Typically, this style fused together all kinds of things, of animal, human and vegetable origin, liberally mingled with creatures such as fauns, nymphs, satyrs and centaurs. Of course the designs were never meant to be underground, but their rediscovery in the dark tunnels and rooms of buried palaces and bathhouses lent the term that first came into common use to describe them – *grottesche* – an entirely subterranean feel.*

It was a shock for the purists to discover this rogue element in classical art and so from the beginning the term took on a bigger role, representing any perceived deviation from the morally and aesthetically acceptable. The Gothic Revival in the nineteenth century fused it with medieval architectural carvings, which similarly perplexed viewers. Grotesque, however, is always recognisable to some degree. If we can't put a name to the monster we can at least describe what it's made out of – a bird's wing, a lion's claw, a snake's body, a man's head – and so on. It is definable and indefinable at the same time. One of my favourite books on the subject, Geoffrey Galt Harpham's *On the Grotesque* (1982), suggested that 'Grotesqueries'

both require and defeat definition: they are neither so regular and rhythmical that they settle easily into our categories, nor so unprecedented that we do not recognise them at all. They stand at a margin of consciousness between the known and the unknown, the perceived and the unperceived, calling into question the adequacy of our ways of organizing the world, of dividing the continuum of experience into knowable particles.

* *La grottesca* and *grottesco,* the Italian roots of the word, both refer to *grotta* (cave), which is related to the Latin *crypta* (crypt) and the Ancient Greek *kryptos* (hidden).

Harpham goes on to suggest that grotesques are the 'things left over when the categories of language are exhausted'; they are a defence against silence when 'other words have failed'.

I loved this interpretation and its relevance to medieval religious buildings struck me immediately, for they too seem to occupy and define the spaces at the edges of the known world, where the everyday and the divine might mingle. I realised that medieval sculpture, so often composed of grotesque elements, was poorly understood – not because its images were inherently meaningless but because they carried an excess of meaning, which placed them at the limits of understanding. This was, for me, a heady and exciting discovery.

But this was theory and suddenly I was in a world of practice. If I had some understanding of this type of imagery I had much less of the craftsmen who had made it. Now, however, I was looking at their work on a daily basis, working alongside it, beginning to see patterns. A name started to appear with increasing frequency: William of Montecute, a sculptor active in the early fourteenth century.

On the trip back across the Fal estuary the water was choppier than on the journey out, and a note of cold had crept in as the early evening brought a layer of cloud. It was just past six o'clock when we disembarked from the ferry but it seemed like a different town to the one I'd left only a few hours before, deserted and shadowy, and my footsteps echoed loudly as I walked back to my flat. I'd left the fallen books from my hurried departure this morning in a stack by the door. Negotiating my way past I noticed that among them were some about the cathedral so I scooped them up, made myself a cup of tea and sat down to look through. The cathedral had been in the back of my mind for the best part of the day – I still worried whether leaving the job was the right decision – so this seemed appropriate, as if these images wanted to be looked at again, as if I'd unconsciously made this accident happen.

Of all the carvings in the cathedral the strangest must be a man sat on the back of a goat, naked apart from a hat and a mesh or net draped over his body. He faces forwards but twists his head to look behind, holding the goat's tail with one hand and one of its horns with the other. The scene is surrounded by the rippling leaves characteristic of the early 1300s, a favoured framing device of contemporary carvers which, in a roof-boss world, adds a note of normality. And it is – though what passes for normal in the decorated bosses of the vaulted Gothic ceiling at Exeter (and in many other cathedrals and churches), among the mermaids and dragons and Green Men, is of course, far from ordinary.

Roof bosses are found where the ribs in a vaulted ceiling meet. This particular one, of the goat and semi-naked rider, had caught my attention one day – as it was no doubt meant to do. I got on with the day's work and forgot all about it. But as I got to know them better this one would be one of the few that stood out, oddly enough not so much because of the image but for the possibility that it might be able to be identified as the work of one man.

For the most part craftspeople in the medieval period are anonymous and their names unrecorded. Exeter Cathedral, however, is fortunate in that it has a rich documentary resource in the Fabric Accounts, a record of payments for work that covers much of the period of the Gothic rebuilding. Listed here are the wages paid to carpenters, glaziers, labourers and stonemasons, and among them the name 'William of Monteacuto' appears a few times in the early part of the fourteenth century. A stonemason and sculptor from Montacute in Somerset, he is interesting for lots of reasons. First, this was an exciting time for stonemasons. Some of them were beginning to become sculptors rather than all-purpose masons expected to turn their hand to anything, from fixing stone to decorative carving. A mason was generally referred to as *cementarius* or *lathomus* in medieval Latin, but during the late thirteenth and early fourteenth centuries the terms *imaginator* or *imager* appear, used to refer to carvers and sculptors. It is difficult to isolate the moment at which sculptors emerged as specialists, distinct from stonemasons. For the most part, their work would have continued to include both, but the evidence seems to suggest that by about

1300 figure sculpture was becoming a separate branch of the craft for which a specialist might be employed.

The emergence of sculptors as professionals reflected the wider social context in which patrons of building projects, from cathedrals to chapels and other monuments, required skilled workers capable of producing images. From the pattern of payments recorded in the accounts it is clear that William had a degree of flexibility in his working life, which is likely to have made him one of these early, independent, stone carvers. Beyond that, however, one reference records the subject of one of his carvings, and from this it might be possible to identify not only which one it is but also some of the others that he worked on.

In the evenings after work I'd started digging into the literature and quickly realised that I was not the first to try to identify William's sculptures. In 1910, it was suggested that he was responsible for the 'eight exquisite vaulting-shaft corbels of the presbytery, and the bosses in the roof of the same.' Then in 1935 H. E. Bishop, more plausibly, suggested that these corbels were by Roger, the master mason from the late thirteenth century until 1310, proposing instead that William was responsible for the doors to the choir and five corbels within it. Bishop also introduced the idea that the head at the base of the corbel at the south-west corner of the choir, which also features St Catherine, was that 'of a mason with a cap and probably his own portrait'. Charles Cave, writing in 1953, agreed:

> William of Montacute seems to have been the actual carver of presbytery and quire bosses and corbels. It may well be that we see his portrait on the corbel on the south side of the quire under the figure of St Catherine, and it is perhaps no accident that she and the master carver should thus appear together, for the church at Montacute in Somerset, whence William came, is dedicated to St Catherine.

This talk about portraits was off-putting; in how many churches does the guide booklet tell you that the generic crowned heads among the architectural sculpture are Edward III or Queen Eleanor of Aquitaine? But this was different, I was part of this world now, and I wanted to find out more about this character, who, in a distant way, was a craft ancestor of mine.

The reference that had provoked my interest hinted at the content of two of his carvings. In 1312, there is a payment to William:

Week 4   In wages of William de Monteacuto carving one great
corbel one great boss and 2 bab[wins?] at task.

What were '2 bab'? The most likely interpretation is, as the editor of the accounts suggested, a shortened form, and early recorded use of, the term *babewyn*.

Babewyn or *babwin* is a precursor to the word 'grotesque', a word that medieval people themselves would have been aware of (Chaucer, for example, uses it in his poem *The House of Fame*). It is significant that, while the term was used to refer to all manner of creatures, its origin is with the ape or monkey (from *babuini*, the source of the word 'baboon'). By 1312, when the reference to the carving of '2 bab' by William appears, work at Exeter had reached the transept area, joining the new Gothic work to the Romanesque north and south towers and then continuing westwards into the east end of the nave. In this location, and with the above reference in mind, there are two small carved capitals of this date that stand out. They are tucked away, high up at clerestory level on the south side of the very east end of the nave: one carved with a haltered bear, the other with an ape riding on the back of a hound. It is the only carving in the cathedral to feature an ape. Are these the '2 bab'? Certainly, they are playful grotesques, but only one represents an ape, the original source of the word. This ape is also a mimic: closely copying a boss from ten years before, a time when William was a salaried employee of the cathedral.

It was in this period that the corbels and bosses of the presbytery vault were carved, painted and fixed. This is where the naked goat rider occurs, or to give him a name: Marcolf, the trickster, the fabled sharp-minded peasant widely known from medieval literature. Marcolf was a medieval folk hero famous for his frank yet comedic exchanges with King Solomon. The dialogue of witty one-liners and acerbic put-downs, riddles and tales, enjoyed an extraordinary popularity in the later medieval period. The boss at Exeter illustrates the tale in which Marcolf is told to appear before the king neither riding nor walking, neither on horseback nor on foot, neither naked nor clad, neither barefoot nor shod and so on. The apparently impossible conditions are solved by arriving on the back of a goat, trailing one foot along the ground, naked except for a net. In its picturing of the paradoxical, it is an image which speaks of nothing being as it seems, of having entered a world turned on its head.

The features shared by this boss and the simian *babewyn* in the transept, carved a decade later, include the odd composition (man riding a goat; ape riding a hound); the pose of the riders (one hand on the horn or head of the animal, the other on its rear or tail, and the head tilted backwards), and, to a certain degree, the shape and undulations of the foliage. One feature of particular interest is the head of the rider. His neatly groomed beard, the sides of the face shaved close, and hair ending in a curl at the nape of the neck, the whole topped off with a cap, are nearly identical to that of the head at the base of the corbel carved with St Catherine at the south-west end of the choir. Of all the work identified with William, it is the large corbels of the choir and transepts which have regularly been attributed to him, and of these it is this one featuring the 'portrait head' which was first identified in 1935.

Perhaps these carvings are his, though the evidence is far from conclusive. There is a style, a general feel that it is easy to cleave towards, and I'd like to think that these three carvings – the ape and hound, Marcolf and goat, and St Catherine are the work of William of Montacute. The close resemblance of the head at the base of the St Catherine corbel with the head of the rider on the earlier Marcolf boss, itself a possible source of inspiration for the ape and hound carved a decade later, display strong stylistic and thematic links. They are also quite unusual images within the architectural sculpture of the cathedral. It seems that not only was William a skilled and inventive fourteenth-century stonemason and sculptor, but one with a leaning towards satirical humour and subversive folktales. If we could ever leap across the six hundred years that separate us and meet up, I have a sense that we'd get on.

Church of the Storms

The slab was the first thing in the van. A piece of Irish limestone about three feet by one foot by three inches thick. Probably the heaviest single thing I owned: I could just about lift it. I've moved enough times since carving it to know that it goes in first, sandwiched by double-thickness cardboard. Everything else can pile on top and I know it'll be alright even though it's one of my most treasured pieces, carved with a repeating Romanesque star design that always seems to look new.

I was moving into a friend's spare room. My place in Falmouth had turned out to be not just damp but wet. There had been a few warning signs. The sea mist that came in through the closed windows. The warped folder of drawings I'd picked up one afternoon that started to drip. The carpet that oozed around my toes. The metal picture frame that had rusted on the wall. The only thing left was to get out, put everything in storage and move into Matt's house across town.

As I heaved the stone into the back of the van I remembered how I'd found it: in a skip at a monumental masons' yard. It took a fair amount of shifting of other offcuts to reach it, the single, pale-grey corner that had initially caught my eye gradually increasing in size as I got closer. It wasn't a perfect rectangle. One of the ends was at a slant, and there was a vent along one side, presumably the reason why it was discarded in the first place. Being sawn on six sides, there were no rough surfaces, though there were a few chipped edges. Otherwise it was a good find.

As I would discover, Kilkenny limestone is a lovely stone to work.

It's hard but cuts cleanly. It holds edges well – it will chip rather than crumble. The colour is the thing, though: cut it and it's pale grey, polish it and it goes a glassy black, like marble. (In fact, it's often called Kilkenny marble.) For several months I wondered what to do with that stone until a trip to a Romanesque church in Herefordshire showed me the way. It was the lintel to the south door at St Andrew, Bredwardine, which became a lesson in the possibilities of repeated geometric patterns. The Bredwardine lintel is carved with one giant rosette or hexafoil motif similar to those on the Cornish fonts at Altarnun, Warbstow and so on. This one, however, was divided so that each spoke or petal crossed a dividing line into an outer ring. Between each point in the outer circle there were smaller circles, each one containing a four-pointed star. On either side of the rosette the remaining space of the lintel was carved with massed star patterns. The design even carried on underneath. Look at it long enough and new patterns were formed from the building blocks of each square. It was an incredible piece of work, showing the potential of simple motifs and their repetition.

Not long after that visit I started to carve test pieces of star motifs on different offcuts of stone, just to get the pattern into my hands. Then, once I was confident, I set out the design on the slab. Star ornament is relatively straightforward to set out. First, you only really need a square with two diagonal lines crossing in the middle to work from. Each quarter, which is a right-angled triangle, becomes a shallow, sunken, unequal-sided pyramid, in effect, as you carve each face at the same angle. Do this for each quarter, twelve faces in all, and you have one four-pointed Romanesque star. Second, the design is flexible enough to fit all manner of imperfectly sized stone. So long as a four-sided shape can be drawn onto it, or squeezed into a corner, it is possible to produce a star motif.

On my slab I intended to do thirty of approximately similar size, in three rows of ten. The slight angle at one end of the slab could be accommodated by stretching the design; one point of some stars would appear slightly longer than the others. I thought that would look good: human, imperfect and purposeful ('Good sculpture is purposeful,' as John once said to me. 'You may not know what its purpose or meaning is, but you can feel its presence.')

I carved it in my friend Rosie's studio on the edge of Dartmoor over several months, a day here, a day there, whenever I could find the time. I averaged about three to four stars per visit. 'Edge' of Dartmoor doesn't really do the location any justice – the gate to the moor is right next to it, a former barn now carpeted in white marble dust and stacked with pieces of stone: Portland, Carrara, Spanish alabaster. Sometimes I'd cycle there from where I lived in Ashburton, taking a short cut through the grounds of Buckfast Abbey and up the ridiculously steep hills behind Scoriton and Combe, several miles of gradient. It seems to me that where you make something is almost as important as the making itself. The studio, remote and at the end of an unsurfaced road, the weather, my journey there, the conversations we had, all went into the stone in some way, which itself drew from the long heritage of decorated lintels, grave slabs and other architectural sculpture. Centuries of working practice, not to mention daily life, live in each project.

While sculpture, like other artistic practices, can bend itself into the shapes of words, it takes its life from the sensory realms beneath and beyond them. These 'empty spaces where art happens' are impossible to quantify. It can be difficult to know, let alone explain, the feelings a work inspires, not just during its making but in the life it then takes on when finished, separate to the circumstances in which it was produced. The artist and teacher Philip Rawson believed this was due to the complex connections between memory and sensory experience. Those works of art that resonate with these submerged memory traces are like powerful beams of light illuminating forgotten or hard-to-reach aspects of ourselves.

With each new star carved, the pattern on the stone became more and more complex, new lines and shadows confusing the eye. Some days I'd be dazzled by the thing and unable to focus properly – the apotropaic entrapment theory is far from just an idea. I was particularly excited to finish it. The raw, cut surfaces, textured with my chisel marks, were pale grey. At the edges, where I'd polished it,

the grey deepened to a charcoal black. The American author Richard
Sennett, writing about the emotional rewards of making something
in his book *The Craftsman*, notes that the process of engaging with
a given material means that 'people are anchored in tangible reality,
and they can take pride in their work.' Connecting with tangible
reality is the lightning rod that brings us out of the ether and fully
into the here and now, with all its complex and conflicting emotions.

Once the carved slab had been loaded and wedged with other
stones, I started to pack in the boxes of books. My books had been
the real tragedy of the flat. Once pristine, they were now warped or
buckled from damp. As with stones, I'm heavily invested in books.
I can generally remember how they've made their way into my life;
where I bought them, who gave them to me, how I met the author.
Some of them are associated with loss. All the different moments
and emotions that the physical form of a book contain are woven
into my own personal history. This repository of connections means
that not only are they irreplaceable but the casually inflicted damage
felt like a personal attack. In the second chapter of their book *Stuff*,
the authors Randy O. Frost and Gail Steketee consider how owning,
or collecting belongings, defines who we are:

> In some early civilizations possessions were seen as part of an
> individual's "life spirit" or self. Anthropologists have proposed this as
> the basic psychological process for ownership, which can be refined
> by cultural factors. Among the Manusians, an island tribe in Papua
> New Guinea described by Margaret Mead in 1930, this belief was
> readily apparent. They held possessions to be sacred and grieved for
> things lost as they would for lost loved ones.

I can understand that. The narratives that live in an object, whether it's
a building, a book or a sculpture, give us life. Through the experience
of looking at it or reading it or living in it or visiting it, we become
part of its story as much as it becomes part of our own.

The fate of historic carved stones, like that of my books, often
hinges upon one person's decision or actions. In 2004, for example,

a section of a Romanesque capital was chiselled off from the chancel arch at All Saints in Buncton, West Sussex. The image that was removed in this act of twenty-first-century iconoclasm was that of a 'sheela-na-gig', a figure often found on medieval churches in Britain and Ireland. Sheela-na-gigs are carvings of female figures, often hunched or squatting and usually completely naked, their genitals exaggerated. The pagan revival of the twentieth century adopted them as fertility figures, and it is under this cloak of twentieth-century occultism that they are best known, rather than as part of the rich visual world of medieval Christianity. Regardless, someone took exception – either to the pagan narrative foisted upon them, or perhaps to the representation of a naked body in a church – and chiselled the figure into pieces. It had been undisturbed since the twelfth century.

In 2013 I discovered that another carved Romanesque stone, this time one from Devon and one that I knew well, had mysteriously disappeared. I'd first seen the piece in a short note, 'Two Norman Tympana in South Devon', published in the 1977 issue of the Devonshire Association's *Transactions*. In this, the author E. N. Masson Phillips had photographed and described two carved stones: one in the churchyard at St Budeaux near Plymouth, carved with a sunken circular panel in which a cross had been cut, and the other in Dawlish, above a garden gate. This second one of the two was carved with repeating palmettes, three large ones in a row, beneath an arch of star designs. Even in the grainy black-and-white photo that accompanied the piece, I could see that it was likely to be by the same workshop responsible for a particular group of south Devon fonts.

Kate Clarke had called this group of Romanesque fonts the 'honeysuckle' fonts, owing to their shared design of a repeating palmette – or as she preferred, honeysuckle – motif. The ornament, based upon classical examples of a stylised foliate frond, was often used for architectural decoration in Greek and Roman temples. In Romanesque Devon it had crystallised into a kind of abstract foliage burst with two small volutes, the whole contained within an oval and linked to its neighbour by a pointed leaf-like spike. Like the geometric designs, it had some degree of flexibility as well as being aesthetically pleasing, either being used on its own to fill a small space or joined up to create a running band. Perhaps this was why the carvers of the twelfth century took to it with such enthusiasm: it was a useful image in their toolkit of motifs. Honeysuckle. As descriptive terms for medieval carvings go, it's one of the more immediate ones, conjuring hot days and luxuriant, sweet-smelling foliage, and as such entirely appropriate that it should be so strongly associated with the warm red sandstones of south Devon on which so many of them appear.

Twelve of these fonts survive in rural churches in Devon.* I'd fallen under their spell one summer. It wasn't enough to just seek them out, though I had, heading out at weekends on my bike beneath uncertain weather and on unforeseen gradients into the heart of the South Hams, that triangle of Devon between Plymouth, Kingsbridge and Exeter. Sometimes I needed to sit and carefully draw the motifs too, noting the number of leaves – usually four or five – of each palmette. In this way I got to know each carving well, from the fire-blackened and asymmetrical example at Buckfastleigh, to the regular and neat ornamentation at Cornworthy. At first glance these fonts had appeared the same, or at least similar. But close scrutiny revealed that beyond the simplicity there was a playful complexity. Each font had its own character. A repeated pattern had become, in the hands of these unknown and long-dead masons, a kind of music with its own cadences and unexpected phrasings. I drew them. I painted them. I carved one, in a piece of coarse Bath stone, a stilted and stiff attempt to try and understand the design.

Some of the honeysuckle fonts belonged to churches close to rivers, suggesting that moving these heavy and awkward bits of stone was made considerably easier by boat. Still navigable by seagoing vessels up to Totnes, the River Dart may well have been used to deliver finished or near-finished pieces to Dartmouth, Cornworthy and Ashprington, for example. Thurlestone is on the coast. At

---

* Ashprington, Blackawton, Buckfastleigh, Cornworthy, Dartmouth (St Petrox), Denbury, Paignton, Plymstock, South Brent, Thurlestone, Ugborough and Wolborough (Newton Abbot). Outliers, connected to this group but with different designs, include the fonts at Dean Prior, Harberton, Loddiswell, Dittisham, South Pool and Rattery.

other sites such as Ugborough and South Brent the Avon or the Erme could have been used, at least for part of the journey. In later centuries transport by water was still important. During the Gothic rebuilding of Exeter Cathedral, for example, roughed-out bosses of Portland stone, worked at the coastal quarries in Dorset, were taken by sea and up the River Exe to Exeter. Transportation of stone is still an important consideration and a determining factor in its cost, as it probably always has been. The fewer miles travelled the better, although the status of some stones and the workshops that carved them, such as our palmette carvers, may have meant that customers were willing to pay more to have one delivered greater distances.

Scattered throughout south Devon there is an alternative form of the palmette motif. Again, these appear chiefly on fonts. They don't appear to be linked to the red sandstone ones and quite likely were carved by different stonemasons. They are a different shape, known as a 'girdled tub' font, essentially a cylinder pinched at the midpoint or slightly higher to form a 'waist', which is itself defined by a run of cable ornament. Upper and lower sections are both carved. These fonts, found at Farringdon, West Anstey, Buckland-in-the-Moor, Bishopsteignton, Cheriton Bishop, Coffinswell and Combeinteignhead are carved in Beer stone, the pale-coloured, chalky limestone from the south-east of the county. Here the palmette appears as a rounded leaf lacking volutes, but still contained within a small oval. At Ideford there is a tympanum on which this variety of palmette appears between a dragon and a richly plumed bird.

These clearly defined groups of fonts and other carvings, each with characteristic traits and common features, might tell us something about the way in which these stonemasons worked. For one, the restriction of particular motifs to particular stone types (the 'sharp' pointed leaf style on the work in New Red Sandstone; the rounded 'soft' leaved style on the Beer stone carvings) suggests that as early as the twelfth century, small localised groups of carvers were working directly at the quarry locations themselves, producing short editions of standardised yet highly distinctive pieces. That they were not replicated in greater numbers is likely due to the large number of small quarries active at the same time, this activity not being conducive to long production runs and lines of evolution. Given that stone is difficult to move and messy to work, this would have also served a practical purpose: minimising the transport of waste (stone that would have to be removed as part of the carving process). From later centuries there is documentary evidence for such working practices. William of Montacute, for example, regularly completed 'task work' off-site at the quarries at Ham Hill near Yeovil.

The tympanum was important as it showed that this group of stonemasons had carved something other than fonts. Through doing some research I'd discovered that the first notable event in its post-medieval life had taken place in 1808, when it was engraved for the *Antiquarian and Topographical Cabinet*, a popular series of early nineteenth-century books on the landscape, buildings and topography of the British Isles. It was an important image since it showed the tympanum *in situ*, before the restoration of the church. There was some artistic licence but overall it was a fairly accurate engraving. Crucially, it showed other carved stones that had been lost. The description beneath the image ran:

This porch, of which a Plate is given, has an ornamented arched entrance. The outer circle of which is a double band of twisted foliage springing from grotesque heads; beneath this circle is another arch of plain stones, the internal part of which is ornamented in basso-relievo with trellis-work and zigzag; and under this are stones richly embossed with volutes, which extend across the door-way.

The stones 'richly embossed with volutes' were the three large palmettes carved on what is in fact one piece of stone, the palms beneath an arc of star designs and saw-tooth chevron. During the restoration of the church in the early 1820s, the tympanum was moved from its position above the north door to a house up on the cliffs at nearby Dawlish, being built by the Reverend Charles Phillot, curate at the time. Here it remained undisturbed over 'a garden door leading from the road into a shrubbery,' as the *Transactions* piece stated.

I wondered why Phillot had removed the piece. Was it an act of rescue, the tympanum otherwise heading to the early-nineteenth-century equivalent of the skip?* It's uncertain if its position above a garden gate, where it had been since at least the 1970s, was its original placing. If so, then perhaps he saw it as simply a nice addition or backdrop to his planting, much like the cast statues of classical deities and animals that can be bought at garden centres today. Whatever his reasons, however, he did a good job, and possibly saved it from destruction. It was a substantial and important example of Romanesque sculpture by the Torbay/Teignmouth school of masons, that had largely disappeared over the past two centuries.

Not long before I left Exeter for Falmouth, I'd set out to find it. I had an Ordnance Survey map and the *Transactions* piece with me, and hoped that between them that would be enough. After a lot of walking around, it dawned on me that the gate with the blue door that I had passed several times must be it. There was a familiar low triangle shape above it. Was it really that easy?

I knocked on the door to the house. A woman with dark, shoulder-length hair answered. I introduced myself and explained why I was there. Her response was unexpectedly hostile.

'How do you know about it?'

'It's a loved piece of sculpture – people have written about it. Look.' I handed over my photocopy.

'Where did you get this?'

'From the library.'

'I'll take a copy of that. Who are you again? I don't want you writing about it.'

As we walked with some difficulty through an overgrown part of the garden, she asked me whether it was valuable and how much it was worth. I said it was unique, which it was. But also that I doubted whether it was worth anything financially. Its value lay in its remarkable

---

* However, the survival of numerous twelfth-century corbels from the original church suggests that carved stones were kept. These carved corbels, mentioned in a description of the church in 1793, have survived inside the tower set into the wall and are whitewashed the same as the masonry. There are birds and a snake biting its tail, beast heads with strange, scooped-out eyeballs, some geometric motifs that include a volute – these may well be by the same carvers.

survival, here, not far from where it was created in the first place. The piece was hidden beneath brambles, holly and ivy. I took some awkward photos, propping up long sections of creepers with my head

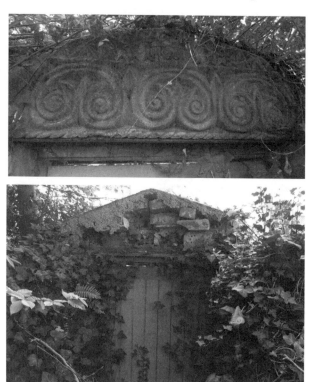

to keep them away from the stone. I could see that it was discoloured by growth of some kind but was, overall, in good condition. I thanked the woman and left, pleased to be on my way.

Two years later, when developers took over the house and garden, the eight-hundred-year-old sculpture was discovered to be missing, prised from where it'd been set. Its whereabouts are still unknown.

All night the rain had kept me awake with its furious clattering on the windows, each fresh gust hammering the house to its bones. 12.30; 2.46; 3.33; 5.14; all slipped by, and with the prospect of sleep diminishing, I got up and drew the blinds. Half-past six. The first tendrils of light were seeping through the clouds and there were waves breaking over the harbour wall, white water swallowing its granite arm. Arriving in Penzance the previous evening, I'd dropped my bag at the B&B and gone for a walk. It was the last day of October. The wind had yet to fully bite but already waves were striking the promenade wall, a spray of white water hanging in the air long enough to be blown across the road. I bought some chips and ate them sitting on a nearby bench, safely out of the way and protected from the weather by a wall and a small stand of trees. Three teenagers were running the gauntlet of the prom, shrieking as the exploding waves fragmented into droplets above them. Under the streetlights the white water lit up like ultraviolet.

The morning light brought fresh evidence of the night's destruction, though the storm had yet to abate. Mounds of black seaweed had been flung across the seafront road, and here and there fallen branches with worried, twittering leaves were pushed up against parked cars. Upstairs in the Morrab Library I watched as each new gust flattened the shrubs in the gardens outside. I'd blown in through the front door and struggled to close it behind me. 'Isn't it fantastic?' said the woman tidying the books for sale immediately next to the door. 'Yes,' I replied, 'it's everything I'd hoped for.'

I'd come to Penzance to do some research. Years ago, on a quick visit to Cornwall, I'd visited a small church that stood, amazingly to me, on the beach. It seemed to sum up everything that I understood about the South West then – the mysterious quality of the place. I wanted to find out more about this church on the sands at Gunwalloe, a building so perilously close to the unfettered rage of the Atlantic that it was known locally as the Church of the Storms.

The Morrab Library is a wonderful place to sit out a storm. Founded in 1818, it occupies Morrab House, a Victorian mansion set within a landscaped garden of palms and ponds that slopes gently down to the sea. It's one of the few independent libraries still left in the country, with diverse collections on all manner of subjects. I gathered up the usual suspects from the architecture and Cornish history shelves (Pevsner, Sedding) and headed upstairs to the best seats in the house, where the view offered me flashes of sunlight through broad, wet leaves and a glint of rolling waves in the distance.

The church of St Winwaloe at Gunwalloe, is, according to the updated Pevsner volume on *Cornwall,* located in 'an especially romantic site for a church, on its own on the edge of a sandy cove but sheltered from the sea by a bluff.' Without this giant rock and its attendant spikes of slate to break the waves, the building probably wouldn't have lasted much more than one Cornish winter. 'So close is the building to the shore,' wrote the vicar in 1870, 'that the waves have frequently broken away the walls of the churchyard.' Its origins are – perhaps suitably for a building that sits alone on a stretch of sand hills (or towans) and dramatic eruptions of rock, flanked by unstable cliffs – obscure, prey to fanciful narratives. In *The Churches and Antiquities of Cury and Gunwalloe in the Lizard District,* published in 1875, Alfred Hayman Cummings mentions a local tradition about two sisters who vowed to build a church if they escaped from their wrecked boat with their lives. They survived, so the tale goes, but couldn't agree upon the site, and finally settled their differences by agreeing that one sister should build the tower and the other the nave and chancel, which rather too neatly, perhaps, explains the unusual separate structures.

Cornish antiquary and artist John Thomas Blight (1835–1911) also mentions this story of the church being built 'as a votive offering by one who here escaped from shipwreck,' but gives an alternative explanation:

> It is said that the builders intended to erect the church on higher ground, nearer the centre of the parish, at Hingey; but as fast as materials were brought to the place they were, by some mysterious agency, removed during the night to the present site. And here the church was built, it being found useless to contend with a supernatural power.

This supernatural story is a reminder that this coastline is entwined with death and misfortune. On my previous visit I'd spent some time looking at the gravestones and other memorials in the small churchyard. One of them recorded the final resting place of an unknown Luftwaffe pilot. A particularly beautiful stone near the porch, Italian marble set with a piece of slate, read 'Remember Adam and Rachael Watson who died on 8th December 1998' in hand-cut letters, neatly spaced between a carved sprig of oak leaves and a heavy-headed sunflower. The design was a simple one, but the work that had gone into it was considerable. I found myself wondering about the healing power of stone and how its use as a memorial might anchor grief in time and place, and in this way help those left behind to find a way through. In commemorating and connecting with the lost, thoughts and memories become a bridge between life and death.

The branch of a tree scraped against the window, breaking my reminiscence. The storm seemed to be getting worse. A fellow library user appeared to tell me that he'd just heard they were going to close. As I started to pack up, a librarian confirmed that a tree had come down in the gardens and the grounds were now closed to the public. Given that the library was part of these it had to close too. I gathered my things and headed out into the rain.

I sheltered in a nearby café and studied the image from Cummings's book on my phone: a sepia photograph of St Winwaloe's Romanesque font, which, at that point in time (the latter part of the nineteenth century) was a fairly sorry-looking thing propped upon a section of column. Its upper part was missing a crescent of stone, like a bite mark from some unknown creature, and it was still in this state when Sedding drew it over thirty years later (he described it as being 'in a mutilated condition on a shelf at the west end of the church'). Reading Blight as I had just done, however, I'd learned that this situation was in fact a step forward in terms of the font's preservation, for it was previously to be found in the churchyard, yet another piece of Romanesque sculpture moved, perhaps when the new font was installed in the later medieval period, then salvaged and returned to the church.

Walking through the rain meant that I'd missed a call. Back in my B&B I saw that it was my old friend from college, Tom. I called him back. He was working on a manor house on the Wiltshire-

Dorset border, built of greensand ashlar that was in need substantial repairs and stone replacement. Could I help him for a week or two? I could. Arrangements made, I told him I'd been writing about Weymouth College.

'Oh okay. What kind of writing?'

'Just trying to remember how we managed to learn what we did, and how'.

'It was a bit, um, interesting at times wasn't it? Remember the acanthus leaf?'

'Yes! Have you still got yours? Mine blew up. I've glued it back together though.' Not only had I glued it back together but I'd filled the cracks and painted them the same colour as the glaze. It looked almost new. The acanthus leaf was a maquette and was meant to be a timed exercise, to replicate potential working conditions. The original plan was that we'd have just half an hour to take all the measurements and photos that we needed. In the end, our collective ineptitude drove Chris to despair, and he propped the acanthus up on the table next to us. But the point was made: get the details that you need and get them quickly. We fired our clay models in the art department's kiln – an afterthought. We hadn't prepared the clay for firing so many of them fell apart, mine included.

'Mine didn't blow up but did disappear,' Tom said. 'At my ex-wife's house. Turns out she'd balanced it on a windowsill and it fell off one day and broke. First I knew about it was finding the pieces in the bin. It was upsetting. No wonder we got divorced.'

In the perpetual cycle of loss and recovery we rediscover what is important about that thing, over and over, again and again. Usually it's an emotional connection, a place where a part of us has rested and been held for a moment, long enough to be absorbed into that object. Certainly if we've made it ourselves: there is a fragment of self-revelation lodged within it, of just what we are capable of doing. This magical connection between things and self is an important one. Objects maintain identity by preserving personal history (and in their making: if you carve a stone you and the stone are connected, from the 'unparalleled intimacy,' as Batten memorably put it, of head and hand and material). The repair and recovery of a piece of sculpture or a building isn't just a repair for its own sake then, but for a personal or collective sense of identity too, just as its easy loss through carelessness, greed or misunderstanding robs us of something that not only cannot be replaced, but is hard to replace or rediscover in ourselves.

Perhaps this is why I feel that Romanesque sculpture runs in my blood. Whatever quality it had that I seized upon in those months of depression, back in 2003 and 2004, had helped me find a way through. It connected with a part of my brain that still worked. The texture of the stone, the lines and the faces, it contained life, the life that something has if it's made by hand. It had enough to spare, enough to lend me, and I was thankful for it. Learning to carve had been a means of getting closer to this source of whatever it was – an energy, a sense of something bigger than myself – and while this alone hadn't 'cured' me, the possibilities that it opened up had led to new places. I had a new perspective. As time went on, just as I hadn't been aware of wandering into the hinterlands of depression, I was unaware of leaving them behind too. The stones had mediated throughout all this, consistent, silent, but present, companions to whatever else I might have been struggling with.

I'd arranged to meet my friend Charlotte the following day. As we drove out to Gunwalloe it was clear that the previous day's storm had left its mark. There were substantial alterations to some of the nearby cliffs, the exposed soil roped off by a bright-orange strip of emergency fencing that redirected walkers around a section of missing coast path. Sand was piled deep in the porch of the church and it was gritty underfoot inside. A soft light filtered through the windows, absorbed by the granite arcades of the nave. The repair to the Romanesque font, right by the door, appeared to have brought it back into use, as it was fitted with a lead bowl and a new pedestal. Its decoration was straightforward but unusual among Romanesque designs, a repeating pattern of broad arches, each of which sheltered an upward-pointing arrow. What was unusual, though, was that it was only carved around one half.

Sedding had sketched the font and recorded the incomplete
pattern in his drawing, unlike Cummings's photograph which
suggested it went all the way around. Perhaps this was why the
stonemason who repaired the font chose not to continue the design

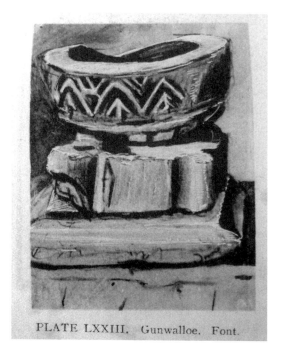

PLATE LXXIII. Gunwalloe. Font.

into the new section of stone but left it blank. It was a good idea,
and the repair as a whole worked well, not just for releasing the font
back into active service but for the skillful and honest indent of new
stone and the balance between decoration and emptiness.

I was reminded of another font, at Fowey, further east, which
illustrated a similar process. As the Gunwalloe font showed, if a
carved stone was otherwise sound but a section of it had failed, one
way to repair it was to chop out the failed piece and insert a new
one. At Fowey, this was exactly what had happened too, though
not without some complications. The font, carved from charcoal
green-black Catacleuse stone and carved with repeating palmette
and star designs, is a genuinely beautiful piece of work – on one side.
On the other, where the large section of indented stone is inserted,

the design is continued well to begin with, but soon abandoned, leaving a blank section. It may have been the case that the carver gave up, quite possibly owing to having left too little space for the final palmette motif that would join the repaired insert of stone to the original medieval design. Alternatively, we might follow the grim imaginings of the church booklet: 'Round the rim of the bowl is a star pattern which is unfinished, usually a sign that the carver died before completing the series.'

In the nave of the church at Gunwalloe we stood as still as possible. It was one of those silent early autumn afternoons where the sky was blank, the quietness amplifying ordinary movements and sounds. Even the sea, just outside, seemed like it was barely moving. I crouched down beside the font to have a closer look at the carving around the bowl, once again impressed by the repair that fitted it so well. Whoever did this had given this piece of stone a new life, rescuing it from sitting propped on another fragment of carving by the wall, as Blight's photograph had shown. It's not all loss then. Loss must be balanced out with examples such as this. If carved stones disappear, are broken, buried, they are also – with luck – found, mended, and reused. Recovery, or at least its potential, hides in each one.

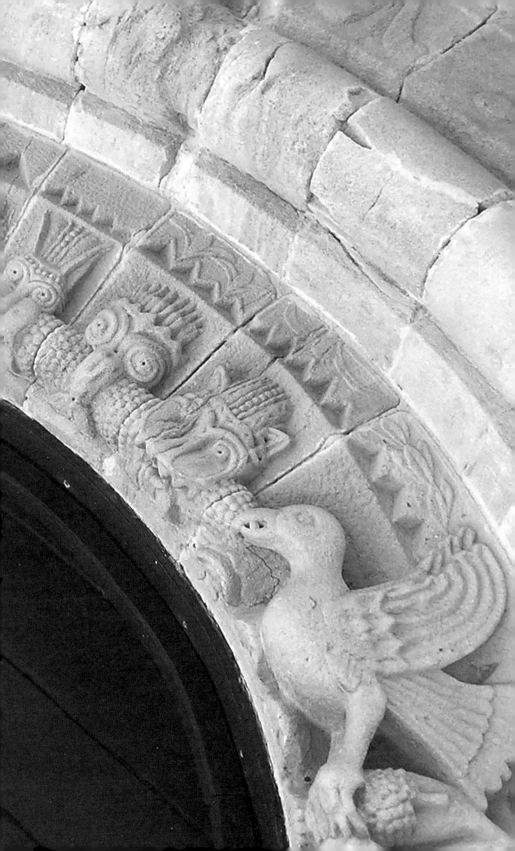

Bird Man

Sorting out what was to go into storage and what would come with me into the spare room at Matt's led to some new discoveries. One of these was a box full of notebooks and papers that I couldn't place so I kept them out, curious to have a look when I had a moment. On a dull day, with the Cornish palm directly outside the window waving about in a strong breeze (its regular cargo of pigeons like joyriders at a funfair), I sat surrounded by a semicircle of articles and photos. Among them were several things of interest, one of which was a photocopied article complete with an impressive close-up photo of a ferocious-looking spider.

If you suffer from both vertigo and arachnophobia, working as a stonemason – at least at Exeter – is not for you. At height on the cathedral we regularly found the secretive and beautiful, velvet black and green-fanged *Segestria florentina* or tube web spider. It has a fondness for decaying stone, making its home in silken funnels in holes or cracks; however, it would prefer that the stone remained that way, so will wander off if disturbed. They have a bite like a bee sting. Their venom includes a deadly neurotoxin (deadly only if you are a small insect). They are fast too: tickle one of the trip wires that radiate outwards from their tube home – probably best to use a chisel or something similar rather than a finger – and a dark blur of legs will shoot out only to return just as fast, disappointed to encounter a metal edge and not a meal.

Segestria florentina is a migrant. Originally from the Mediterranean, it was likely introduced to the UK via sea trade – many of the communities of spiders are in port towns or former port towns, such as Exeter. Early recorded examples occur in the South West, in Bristol in 1889 and Plymouth some years earlier. Because they like stone, the cathedral is their natural home, despite our repair work. It is easy to overlook the fact that old buildings are important for conservation of the non-human kind – insects, birds and so on – as much as they are for human history. To them a cathedral is just stones in the air, a cliff face, shelter, and at height relatively undisturbed except by the occasional stonemason. Peace in the centre of a city. I was happy to work alongside these creatures; we were in their world, after all.

The spiders reminded me of the work that had often led me to encounter them. We'd started work on the upper levels of the west front, the section of cathedral above the screen of statues that dominated the main entrances. It included, on the north side, the largest section of original medieval masonry on any west front of any cathedral in Europe. Its survival was incredible for many reasons. While it may look like a harmonious and united architectural whole, the west front at Exeter is in fact composed of many different types of stone and records a long history of interventions, replacements and repairs. In the later fifteenth century significant changes were begun with the addition of a new tier to the originally two-tiered image screen. In the nineteenth century much of the detail on the upper south side was replaced wholesale, the Victorian masons working their new decorative blind arcading and grotesques with characteristic geometric precision. Numerous individual stones, failed or weathered out across the face of the west front, have also been replaced. This is unsurprising considering what the building has had to endure – aside from the weather.

Throughout the eighteenth and nineteenth centuries and possibly earlier, the habit of celebrating November the fifth by lighting a bonfire directly outside the cathedral led to the loss of much stonework. Contemporary accounts record the stones being too hot to touch, and how cleaning up afterwards involved sweeping up great quantities of carved fragments that had broken off because of the heat. This is an extreme example, perhaps, for stone, if it's outside, is always decaying. It is decaying now, as I write, as you turn these pages. Small losses. Rain eroding a grain of sand from the surface of sandstone; the warmth of the sun drawing out moisture and leaving behind its cargo of soluble salts on the surface of limestone. Plants work their roots into cracks; birds build nests. These everyday processes are normal and could only be stopped if there were no weather and no life. Over time, however, problems can result from these tiny actions. A building stands or falls on its success – or failure – negotiating the myriad forces of decay that set in once it is built, as it is being built, even, if materials are stored and transported poorly, before it is built.

On a structure as large as a cathedral, decay occurs at different speeds in different places. At Exeter, the south-west corner that bears the brunt of the prevailing weather, funnelled along Palace Gate, means that the fourteenth-century statues on the south-facing end of the west front are weathered back, almost completely formless in some cases. The more sheltered areas are still at risk, though in different ways. Damp air or mists can affect stone just as badly as slanted rain and gale-force winds, carrying atmospheric pollutants that bond chemically with the stone, darkening it with characteristic black calcium-sulphate crusts.

Nonetheless, despite everything that nature and humans could throw at it, a section of mid-fourteenth-century masonry had just about survived on the northern side of the west front. Ghostly outlines of architectural decoration were still visible, though exposure to over six hundred years of varying atmospheric (and human) conditions had led to the stone flaking and crumbling, and it needed serious attention. There was considerable discussion as to the best way forward. Stone replacement was mooted for a while, until it was realised that, to be effective, not only would numerous stones have to be substituted, endangering the very significance of the work that we were trying to preserve, but that they would also ruin the architectural lines. This was because the wall had weathered back to such a degree that any replacement stones, set to be compatible with the original wall line, would protrude. For the bulk of the work, apart from weathering courses and one or two carved heads, this was clearly not an option. Instead we embarked upon an ambitious programme of mortar repairs.

Anyone working with historic buildings will quickly get to know about lime. Lime is made from calcium carbonate – chalk or limestone – which is quarried, crushed and heated to between eight hundred and a thousand degrees centigrade. At this temperature the chalk breaks down and releases carbon dioxide, leaving behind calcium oxide, or quicklime. Quicklime is highly unstable and will react violently with water, producing a great deal of heat. In recent years there has been a move towards using 'hotlime' mortar mixes, though it is still more frequently used once it has been 'slaked' and cooled by water. This hydrated lime forms the basis of the limes used for mortars, and depending on any impurities present in the original rock will produce different varieties. As a mortar lime, it is effective for many reasons, but chief among them are two. First, it allows moisture to pass through, thereby preventing the build-up of salt deposits in the stone that lead to decay (which we see when stone is set in and pointed up with impermeable cement). Second, it hardens slowly over time, growing interlocking calcite crystals from its calcium-rich matrix, absorbing carbon dioxide, and by doing so gradually turning back into a version of the rock from which it all began – a chalk or limestone. This series of chemical reactions between calcium, carbon and water is known as the lime cycle.

Each morning I would whisk up one or two buckets of mortar made from different grades of Portland dust and lime. This gave us a pale-coloured mix close to the colour of the medieval Beer stone. We used the mortar to strengthen the outlines of the blind arcading, continuing the lines of the arches where they had, in places, almost weathered back entirely. Slowly, layer after layer, and using ceramic T-pin armatures drilled into the stone for stability and strength, an old part of the west front emerged stronger and sharper, the lines of what was once there easier to read. After all the repairs were done we applied a protective shelter coat, a froth of putty lime, Portland dust, black oxide pigment and the crucial ingredient, casein, a milk protein. This bonded any remaining loose surfaces and provided a sacrificial layer of weathering, helping to protect the stone beneath from the elements.

Despite the flaky nature of the stone, our intervention had brought a new definition. It was repair, yes, and the stone was now in much better shape for the next few decades, but also in some sense the creation of an imagined past: a moment when the architectural detail had started to lose its form but was still readable. It had probably never looked exactly like this. We had added a new moment to its long history, one cloaked in the garb of the past.

Time, as revealed by historic buildings, has a strange elasticity. How do we know what something we've never seen new looked like? At what point are we finished with our repairs? Especially with something that has *never* been new: buildings such as cathedrals, which rarely have one builder and resist completion, are in a state of perpetual process, always unfinished yet also always decaying. As we repair one part another slowly crumbles. Inevitably we produce a mirror-like shard of the present, a past that sits comfortably with our own understanding of it. If decay is a doorway into lost centuries then conservation is a kind of spellwork, a murmuring of sacred words over the carefully collected raw ingredients. Old stone becomes new, weathering is temporarily reversed, time slows down and medieval and modern collide, growing into hybrid fragments of pasts old and new. In many respects old buildings are unstable moments in time, both authentic remnants of the past as well as curated, selected, and hence partially fake ones that tells us just as much – if not more – about the present through the choices taken to preserve them.

This ongoing reinterpretation is one of the reasons that historic buildings inspire our imagination. 'The degradation of cultural artefacts,' writes Caitlin De Silvey 'is usually understood in a purely negative vein: the erosion of physical integrity is associated with a parallel loss of cultural information.' Yet these processes of decay also allow us to contribute new stories, and in this way, recover memory and build alternate narratives. Like the pieces of the Berlin Wall that circulated following its destruction complete with certificates of authenticity, historic material can assume new meanings as it passes from one generation to the next, from one person's experience to another's.

If I'd learned anything from looking for Sedding's grave, it was that sometimes you have to go back to places that you've already visited in order to see something. This was certainly true of medieval sculpture, the weathered stones having a tendency to tease the eye, suggesting numerous interpretations. As I replaced the article about the spiders back in the box I found a handful of photographs of the church at Bishopsteignton in south Devon. It was a hot summer's day when I took them, though I couldn't remember which year I'd visited, as the trees and other vegetation surrounding the church looked dry and parched. There were some photos of ruins too, remains of a fourteenth-century chapel, which, judging by the quantity of photos, had clearly delighted me.

Bishopsteignton has one of the richest collections of Romanesque sculpture in the South West of England. My other pictures showed the doorway in its full extent, three orders of ornament with flamboyantly carved beakheads, a fierce bird of prey, chevron, star motifs, figurative capitals and sculpted columns. There is a font with palmette motifs and above the blocked-up south door is a tympanum that depicts the three Magi, as Pevsner puts it 'marching along under arcades, and a figure (possibly the warning angel) dead frontal in a wide pleated skirt. Everything rigidly stylised, of an unconcern with realism to which one is used only in tribal art.'

It was a drawing that first drew my attention to the church. Browsing through the *Journal of the British Archaeological Association* one day back in Southampton, I found a detailed sketch of the Romanesque tympanum folded into the journal. It quickly became clear that the author of the article was a skilled draughtsman, the article's single photograph outnumbered by this and several other energetic sketches in ink and pencil. These provided what the dark photo of the west door didn't, and that was detailed views of the sculpture itself. The writer clearly had a feel for the work and, as I read, a sound understanding of Romanesque architecture in England as well. The author was P. M. Johnston. I would later discover that the initials 'P. M.' stood for Philip Mainwaring, and it soon became clear why, with my research focused on the South West of England, I had not encountered him before: he was a prolific writer on the medieval art and architecture of the Home Counties, but rarely touched on anything as far west as Devon.

I wanted to find out more about Johnston, whose championing of the work at Bishopsteignton had lingered in my mind all these years. Online, I discovered some material about him in the library of the Sussex Archaeological Society in Lewes, East Sussex. I'd need to visit, just as I felt I had to go back and have another look at the church itself.

I climbed the hill towards the high street from the station. It was an exceptionally cold day in early November. The Sussex Archaeological Society library at Barbican House is next door to the castle keep, which appeared severe and foreboding beneath the grey, wintry sky. I signed in, was directed up some creaky stairs, and was soon surrounded by antiquarian books, journals and ephemera in a warren of interconnecting rooms at the top of the building.

Philip Mainwaring Johnston (1865–1936) was elected to the council of the society in 1900. He was an architect and architectural historian, a contemporary of Edmund Sedding to whom, in many ways, his work and his attitudes ran parallel. As Sedding was to Devon and Cornwall, so Johnston was to Surrey and Sussex: an architect with a sensitivity to the past and an eye for detail honed by practical work and knowledge of materials. His seemingly natural ability to draw had developed early on. Some of the sketches of Bishopsteignton were first done in 1879, when he was only fourteen, and while most were redrawn for publication some forty-seven years later one or two weren't, revealing a confidence in line and tone that would come to distinguish all of his work.* Drawing was crucial to his outlook, his practice as an architect and his understanding of medieval buildings.

Johnston's work as an architect matched his output as a writer. He began his practice in London in 1886 and was busy for many years in building new and restoring old churches and houses, chiefly in the Home Counties. He also designed twenty-four war memorials

---

* His daughter, the actress and writer Thea Holme, wrote that 'at the age of ten he obtained permission to draw in the armour department of the Tower of London'.

and became an expert on medieval wall paintings. Perhaps the ultimate accolade for an architect came towards the end of his life when he was appointed Surveyor of the Fabric at Chichester Cathedral in the 1930s. When, in 1932, a series of replacement heads to the corbel-table on the south transept were carved based upon the dignitaries of the day, Johnston was included alongside the Bishop of Chichester and the Prime Minister, Ramsay MacDonald.

An artist by instinct and an architect by training, we might also count Johnston as one of the very early buildings archaeologists, active long before the discipline of buildings archaeology was identified and founded. His championing of Romanesque sculpture fitted well with such a progressive outlook.

The sun had broken through the cloud and lit up the room where I was working. A crow was hopping about on the roof of the building on the other side of the road. A nearby gull watched it carefully for a moment, its beak set at a disapproving angle, before the pair wandered along differing sections of ridge tiles ignoring each other. Then another crow turned up. The gull threw back its head and shrieked, then flew off. Undeterred, the crows paced nonchalantly, continuing with their inspection of the lead gutters.

On my way back to Falmouth the following day, I broke my journey at Teignmouth and caught a bus to nearby Bishopsteignton. During my last visit, about a decade ago, I remember being entranced by the grinning head that peeped between the elongated leaves on the capital to the south side of the doorway, immediate and fresh and contemporary-looking. Those carved on the other side had distanced or eluded me. Now, the opposite was true. They struck me as two of the oddest carvings in Romanesque sculpture. On the outer one stood a figure with hands raised to support the top of the capital, the lower part of his tunic flared outwards like the highly structured skirt of a period drama. On each side there was a heavy-headed flower and a lone volute. The inner capital presented a similarly clothed figure, carved among trees and abstract foliage, flanked by waist-high birds of prey with pointy wings and an enigmatic figure with folded arms. I called him the bird-man. Even by Romanesque standards he seemed an odd figure to have here, on the doorway to the church.

Birds are a strong theme of the west door. Many of the beakheads on the arch were based on bird forms, terminating on the south side in a large eagle or other bird of prey that took up three voussoirs. This is depicted in profile, looking across to the bird-man capital. Birds in Romanesque sculpture in Devon aren't unusual – there is a wonderfully plumed and worried-looking bird on the tympanum at Ideford, for example, accompanying a palmette and a dragon; on the font at South Milton an acrobat leaps backwards next to a bird of prey; at the aptly named Hawkchurch, with which Bishopsteignton is stylistically linked, there is a single corbel with a bird head; the reset corbels inside the Victorian tower at East Teignmouth feature two carved with birds; and there are birds carved on the capitals beneath the crossing at Crediton. But something about this one, with its heavy beak and outsized form, makes it stand out.

As an architect, Johnston could bring a professional opinion to the architectural history of Bishopsteignton church. In the early nineteenth century a number of drastic restorative actions were taken, chief of which was the demolition of the central Norman tower and the building of a new one at the west end of the nave. There were also other, less obvious but nontheless damaging decisions taken with negative consequences for the sculptural works here. The removal of the porch to the south door, in about 1851, was one of these, the result of, as Johnston writes, 'a devastating restoration' which involved the floor of the church being raised several feet to escape damp from water in the foundations. This made the entrance too low to be used and the doorway was blocked up. This exposed the tympanum to the elements for the first time and to this day it remains unprotected.

Johnston recognised the importance of the tympanum and called the carver a 'forgotten genius'. High praise indeed. It is one of only a few carved Romanesque tympana in Devon, and its depiction of the Adoration of the Magi makes it unusual, if not unique, in Britain.

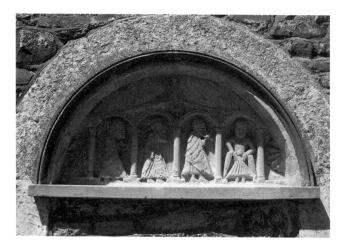

While the imagery appears carved in similar late Romanesque contexts in nearby counties (on the doorways at Malmesbury Abbey in Wiltshire and Glastonbury Abbey in Somerset for instance), as the subject of a tympanum it is a one-off. Johnston, having drawn it, is perhaps the first writer to describe it in any detail:

> The Magi, in profile, advance singly towards the Virgin-Mother, who is seated facing the spectator, under the easternmost arch. She wears a close-fitting cap, and her arms and the figure of the Infant Saviour have been broken away, but the hands, pointing downwards, and one long pendant wrist-sleeve remain … The two foremost of the Wise Kings are bearded, the third is clean-shaven with a cloak over a long tunic, and no head-dress, unless it be a close coif of fur. No. 2 has a sort of low mitre, with a raised band round the brow, and a chasuble-shaped cloak over a tunic. No. 3, who clasps his beard with his hand – a gesture of reverence – wears a dome-shaped fluted helmet, or head-dress, with a rounded rim, and a ball at the top, and a cloak with six pleats or flounces, reminding one of the many-caped coats of our old-fashioned 'cabbies' of days gone by.

On the tympanum at Down St Mary, in work that recalls this, as Johnston noted, there is a similarly clothed figure, with a ribbed garment fastened at the waist much like the Atlas figure on the capital to the north side of the west door. In fact, Johnston drew comparisons between Bishopsteignton and Down St Mary, Hawkchurch and

Sidbury in Devon, and in Sussex, Tortington. He also did something quite unusual for writers on the subject: he attempted a brief, speculative biography of the sculptor.

It is possible that 'if we had any work left of Bishop William Warelwast's Cathedral Church in Exeter, beyond the bases of the transeptal towers' he wrote, 'we should find that this was the true source whence to track our carver.' The likelihood of Exeter Cathedral stonemasons working at Bishopsteignton in the twelfth century is an uncontroversial idea, given the close links between the village and the bishops. But Johnston goes further, imagining our unknown carver finding his first carving jobs in Wiltshire and later, wandering 'into lovely Devon', coming to Exeter with Robert Chichester, the former Dean of Old Sarum (Salisbury) and Bishop of Exeter from 1138 to 1155. If so, he notes, 'the Bishopsteignton capitals and tympanum may have been his swan-song.' This romantic train of thought perhaps reveals more about Johnston's lauded enthusiasm than it does the twelfth century, but it touches on important questions about patronage of sculpture and even the working practices of medieval stonemasons, something still under-explored today.

If the bird man and his companions remained mysterious, their story weathering back into the stone with the rains of each passing winter, enough detail existed to allow the complexity of the work to shine through. As I left the churchyard I realised that this was a serious, high-status doorway, one of the most complex in the South West, surpassing even the work of the period that remains from Exeter Cathedral. It used familiar decorative motifs (star, volute, chevron) that were popular in the work of the nearby Torbay and Teignmouth stonemasons, but used them in uncommon ways. From the figurative capitals, unconventional beakheads and flourishes such as the bird of prey and cartoon-like beast head, it suggested an individual hand – and a highly advanced one at that.

I was coming towards the end of my year-long wanderings around the South West's Romanesque. But I still had two places I wanted to visit. One to see the sculpture I'd read about, the other for the atmosphere that sits at the very heart of Romanesque sculpture.

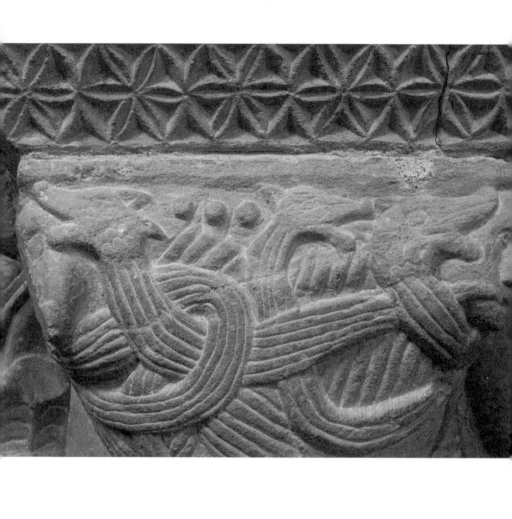

Honeychurch Twilight

In the silence of the cold nave I sat on a pew and tried to remember a quote – one I knew almost by heart in the years when I was writing my thesis. It was a quote by Bernard of Clairvaux (1090–1153), the head of the Cistercian order that had set out to reform the excesses of monastic life. Bernard had protested vehemently against the rich architectural carvings he saw among the capitals of the cloisters and their power to divert the eye of the monks from their books. What was it? Something about monstrous deformities or beautiful monstrosities? I couldn't remember it exactly but found that I had some reception on my phone so looked it up online. It was from a letter written to his friend, William of St Thierry, in the 1120s, and known now as the *Apologia for Abbot William*:

> But apart from this, in the cloisters, before the eyes of brothers while
> they read – what is that ridiculous monstrosity doing, an amazing
> kind of deformed beauty and yet a beautiful deformity? What are the
> filthy apes doing there? The fierce lions? The monstrous centaurs?
> The creatures, part man and part beast? The striped tigers? The
> fighting soldiers? The hunters blowing horns? You may see many
> bodies under one head, and conversely many heads on one body.
> On one side the tail of a serpent is even seen on a quadruped, on the
> other side the head of a quadruped is on the body of a fish. Over
> there an animal has a horse for the front half and a goat for the back;
> here a creature which is horned in front is equine behind. In short
> everywhere so plentiful and astonishing a variety of contradictory
> forms is seen that one would rather read in the marble than in books,
> and spend the whole day wondering at every single one of them than
> in meditating on the law of God. Good God! If one is not ashamed
> of the absurdity, why is one not at least troubled by the expense?

It is a wonderful piece of writing, alive with detail and interest, suggesting that Bernard himself wasn't immune to the power of these images. Beyond the ostentatious display of wealth that sculpted capitals represented, the seductive power of these carvings in the cloister represented, for Bernard, a profound spiritual danger, inviting the sin of mental wandering, or *curiositas*, threatening the activity that lay at the very foundation of monastic life: reading.

On the chancel arch at Hawkchurch was a carved capital that I think would have attracted Bernard's ire, an oddly distracting mix of daisywheels or rosettes, disembodied heads and writhing serpents. I counted the serpents from my seat. There were at least four, each with striated bodies and pointed ears, some of them biting the heads that were carved on the two corners. One even emerged from the mouth of one of these heads. Parts of the background were carved with diagonal lines too, adding to the chaotic intensity of the image, the scored bodies of the snakes appearing to flash and move against them.

Hawkchurch occupies a gap in time, bridges a moment of change: ponderous Romanesque capitals enlivened with bosses and delicate flowers on the north side of the nave, Gothic animal musicians and angels on the south. Outside, there are twelfth-century corbel-tables carved with human and beast heads. It's fortunate that so much has survived, despite the large-scale restoration that took place between 1859 and 1861.

If the daisywheel motif is often linked with an apotropaic, magical ability to ward off evil, to protect whatever it is carved on from the effects of malevolent intent, I wondered if the serpents and the heads here weren't fulfilling a similar role. Heads and masks have been used like this since classical times at least, appearing on terracotta antefixes in temple architecture, sometimes with geometric designs too. Perhaps the repeated masks along the rooflines of Roman temples were the precursors to the tradition of carved corbel tables, themselves sometimes decorated with blank, staring heads, on medieval churches.

As medieval audiences understood, the sacred existed in dangerous proximity to the profane. Monsters in medieval art are often warnings, portents of the unknown, their impossible bodies a bridge between the material and spiritual. This is why they're found in churches, themselves places of overlap between the human and non-human worlds and potentially places of transgress between the two. In this gap there is the opportunity of connection with the divine, but also with danger. If Bernard's main objection to monsters as subject matter for carvings was based on their power to distract the brothers from reading and meditating upon scripture, then, connected to this was the concern that the grotesque forms represented a profound spiritual peril. In this sense, any image presented a potential threat to the monk, for it carried the power to direct attention towards the world of the senses. Every 'sense experience', according to William of St-Thierry, to whom Bernard's *Apologia* was addressed, 'changes the person experiencing it in some way into that which is sensed.' Open the door to the grotesque and it will change you. There is no going back.

The power of the grotesque is closely connected to what it offers, which in essence is a kind of freedom, albeit one where reason has broken down or is about to break down. If disorder and formlessness deprive the mind of the habitual structures necessary for understanding, they also free it from these same restrictions. At the boundary of what is comprehensible is where the grotesque lives and breathes. Bernard was aware of such difficulties of comprehension and offered no easy answers. In his sermons he drew a contrast between *imitatio* (that which can be consumed, appropriated or experienced) and *admiratio* (that which cannot be incorporated in any way). Bernard gave the example of a golden goblet: when it is offered 'we consume, absorb, incorporate the drink (that is, imitate the virtues), but we give back (that is, we wonder at) the goblet.' We wonder 'at what we cannot in any sense incorporate, or consume, or encompass in our mental categories; we wonder at mystery, at paradox.'

Later in the twelfth century, around the time that the Hawkchurch chancel capitals were being carved, another Cistercian was hard at work only five miles or so north, wrestling with profound questions of a different nature. John of Forde, the abbot of Forde Abbey (in what is now Somerset), lived from about 1145 until 1214. A man of insight and prayer, his commentaries on the Song of Songs filled several volumes. In one of these, the bride of the Song uses the image of a craftsman when praising her spouse, and alludes to the work of craft as worth 'lingering a little over'. Reading it recently I wondered if John had observed stonemasons or carpenters directly; I got the sense that he had. The 'craftsman has a chisel in his hand,' he writes,

> and with firmness and great accuracy he brings this to bear on what
> is to be shaped, all his movements controlled by a craftsmanship
> that has become instinctive to him. So the work proceeds with great
> swiftness … so quickly that it outstrips the eye and baffles the mind.

This is human activity entering new territory, where instinct and practice combine to go beyond the human, to meet, as John of Forde would have it, the 'Spirit of God'.

If this is the place where monsters might dwell then maybe it is also the space that artists and makers long for: the perfect balance of practice and instinct. Because they are active in this gap, tools themselves can assume mystical properties, crucial as they are to this transfer of energy from inside to outside, from the interior images circulating around your head to the stone itself. Perhaps bestowing these tools with energy and significance is ingrained into the craft, finding expression in superstition and rituals regarding their use and care. Towards the end of Seamus Murphy's memoir *Stone Mad*, there's a wonderful reminiscence about a 'five-pound penny-faced hammer' owned by 'a quiet inoffensive man who knew a thing or two and kept to his own side of the road'. This hammer had been passed from mason to mason. As Murphy recollected:

> We had its history at our finger-tips; the various men who had
> owned it and taken it all over Ireland and England and America.
> It has worked stone that were only names to most of us – Vermont
> Granite, Indiana Limestone, Elberton Granite from Georgia and
> other American stones; Purbeck Marble, Hopton Wood stone,
> Portland and Clipsham, and Irish Limestones from Ross in Cavan to
> Carrigatrump in Cork.
> We all liked to use it and be thinking of the places and stones it

has seen. Not a day would pass but someone would find a reason to borrow the penny-faced hammer. It was a hammer with personality. If a man was pitching off the over-length on a cross or coping a scantling of limestone he felt it was a job for the penny-faced, which has experience and age and only needed to be shown to the stone.

The week I'd spent working with Tom on the seventeenth-century manor house in Wiltshire had offered a similar insight. Travelling light, I hadn't taken my tools with me; besides, Tom had assured me I could use his. One in particular came alive as I used it, a two-inch claw chisel that sped up an onerous job of trimming away waste stone on the Dorset greensand. I connected with it almost instantly. It was well-balanced and beautifully made, the shoulders of the chisel angled like a faceted jewel. With each use it felt more and more natural. Tom felt no such attachment, though, so he gave it to me and I bought him a new one.

Before I left Hawkchurch I took some more pictures of the capital, clambering onto a chair to get some close-ups. If Romanesque sculpture crystallised in an era of revelatory and apocalyptic fervor around the year 1000, it soon developed into an extraordinary repository of ornament and imagery. It leans towards the otherworldly, relying upon abstraction to lead the mind and the heart into mystery. And always it persists in partial shadow, occupying a place between different worlds, with all the architectural components serving to turn the mind towards contemplation and inner vision.

On the capital, the fading light of late afternoon had worked more shadows into the curves of the creature's bodies, the run of daisywheels flashing like warning lights to the monsters below. Thinking of Bernard's distinction between *imitatio* and *admiratio* I realised that with work such as this, like much of the Romanesque sculpture of the South West, I inclined towards the latter. Even though I might have the skills to be able to imitate it, I wouldn't be able to reproduce its atmospheric qualities. I could only wonder at its mystery, return the goblet, as it were. *Admiratio*.

★

I had one more place to visit before heading back to Falmouth, and that was the church at Honeychurch in mid-Devon. This was somewhere that we'd often visited back in the early 2000s when heading home to Torrington. It is a beautiful place. As the Devon historian W. G. Hoskins wrote, Honeychurch 'has one of the simplest and most appealing interiors of all English country churches.' It lives up to its delightful name in a way that rarely happens, and to see it on a fine morning puts you in a good humour for the rest of the day.

I can understand that. If you told me that Honeychurch was a portal to another dimension, I would probably believe you.

It was the end of a dark December day by the time I found myself walking along the lane to the small building, the light fading fast in the wintry dusk. The church was a simple two-cell building, nave and chancel, with a tower at its west end. The name derived from 'Huna's Church', Huna the name of the Saxon landowner who endowed it with the tithes of his estate. In the eleventh century, the population of the parish was around thirty, pretty much the same as it is today. The five farms mentioned in the Domesday Book – Middleton, Slade, Bude, Westacott and East Town – are still here. There were a couple of Romanesque corbels carved with striking beast heads rebuilt into the wall of the nave, their scored faces and semicircular mouths in stylistic accord with the simple chevron and cable of the font. I wasn't surprised to learn, a few days previously, that John Piper had painted the interior of this unassuming church. There was a similar feeling here to that at Toller Fratrum and some of the other places to which he was drawn. His painting, much like Hoskins's prose, glowed with splashes of warm oranges and golds, the pews leaning away from the carved font as if it were at the centre of a slow-motion explosion. To me, it felt far from dead and inert. In the quiet I sat on one of the pews, its rough texture defined by generations of woodworm.

One of the nicknames my sister gave me when we were teenagers was 'the dusty historian'. It was intended as an insult and delivered when she thought I was being boring, which, to give her credit, was probably most of the time – maybe still is. I can't remember when she first came up with the name even though it was her copy of Peter

Ackroyd's novel *Chatterton* which led me to pick up *Hawksmoor* and *First Light* and then to studying archaeology, a legitimately dusty pursuit. But was dust really all that dull? The 'potential of dust' writes the philosopher Michael Marder, 'is not to be underestimated':

> In addition to letting space appear for a blazing instant illuminated by a ray of light, it warrants a tangible and, indeed, spatial appearance of time. Apart from insinuating that there was something, it also indicates that enough time has elapsed for hair, fur, and dead skin to be shed, for pollen to fly off a tree, for a dying star to be pulverized, or for industrial pollutants, containing silicon, aluminium, calcium, and dozens of toxins, to form copious clouds. Dust measures the lifetimes of animate and inanimate beings and processes, even if it desists from stamping existence with expiration dates and, thus, infinitely defers the final moment of vanishing.

A spatial gauge of time, the reversal of time and space (or the recognition of how closely connected they are) is about as big as it gets: my teenage-self had been right to feel something profound in the archaic. Ruins, fragments, dust, all facilitated a kind of imaginative freedom as well as a profound connection with others, living or dead.

Now I speak ruins, I'm fluent in the language of decay. The years working at Exeter Cathedral have completely reorientated me. How could they not? On a daily basis our conversations were peppered with references to failure and loss: stone spalled and flaked because of the build-up of sulphate crusts, or sheered off owing to incorrect bedding, or broke apart entirely from the accumulated stresses of freeze and thaw. I was part of the cathedral's immune system, intervening when and where necessary to slow the processes that lead to damage and repair parts that had already succumbed. Like the best medicine, our work is more effective when it is preventative, and if we are successful it should be difficult to tell we've been there at all. Like the generations who had come before me, and those who will come after, I had become an anonymous stonemason, my work now a small part of the cathedral's grand narrative. Part of the work of stonemasonry is to accept this strange dichotomy and your place within the order of things, always in the peripheral vision – much like the dust itself. Dust had been there from the beginning, a constant companion to my efforts. Dust, ordinary yet capable, in the right moments, of lending itself to insights of some gravity, was the by-product of my craft.

How much time do we have? It's an unanswerable question. Dust is our future as well as our past. What I did know was that these fonts, tympana, capitals and other carved stones and their churches had weathered through *centuries*. Centuries of rain, wind, damp, changes in style and aesthetics, politics, religion, and with a little help and the odd repair, they were still here. The stones themselves were millions of years older than the images they bore. Seeking these stones out had attuned me to something greater. It didn't matter that the images were sometimes indecipherable and their meanings obscure. It didn't matter that the stones were often broken and split, or partially lost to the weather. They were in a long and ongoing conversation with their surroundings, continually adjusting to new circumstances. Because of this, they still lived.

All stonemasons come face-to-face with the long durations of time on a daily basis. Our work is expected to last hundreds of years, so it has to be good. Yet, by the same token we are often secondary to the original. A stone carved in the 1340s cannot be carved again. Even if it is copied exactly, its circumstances of production have changed, the tools used to carve it have been made differently, and the person carving it is living a different life in a very different world. In replacing a stone it might be argued that different moments in time, then, are what we are really preserving, impossible as that sounds. Perhaps we are recovering traces of events that have occurred in an anonymous life. Through their work we enter a dialogue, and might find ourselves anchored in time and place.

Dusk was gathering, and as the church filled with shadows I was reminded of Richard Sennett's words: we 'become interested in the things we can change.' It is as if working on another material allows a subtle inner transformation to occur, silently and slowly. If learning to work stone had slowly helped me find a way out of the estuarine muds of depression, it had also opened my eyes to the historic material in new and unexpected ways. I could see now that this inflexible, delicate material with a tendency to crumble or break could, in the right hands, become an object of great beauty. Sedding and Johnston both knew this from their detailed drawings, Piper from his paintings, Clarke from her photography. It would seem that the focus offered by an art practice had been crucial in understanding the quality of this work; through carving stone I had begun to be able to see this for myself.

The darkness started to grip the font, highlighting the imperfect geometries of its carved design. This didn't seem to detract, however, from its power. In fact, if anything, it added something, a human presence to an otherwise abstract form. Somebody had been here, carving this, hundreds of years ago. In some sense they were still here, their work speaking for them across the centuries. In a small way, I was part of that world now and they were my colleagues, as Batten had said they would be.

Thinking back on some of my favourite pieces that I'd carved, such as the Kilkenny slab cut with stars, I realised how, in some almost tangible way, the work of doing linked me to my twelfth-century predecessors. The Kilkenny stone had come from Galway, and while Ireland is a relatively unfamiliar land to me, beyond being a tourist, working the stone meant that I now knew its bones. This is strong magic. I grew up in an urban setting, a feeling of detachment perched always on my shoulder, but each carving, and the process of carving, connected me to something. What this was, I wasn't sure. But I had felt a subtle electricity in my veins, the echo of a distant and unquenchable spring.

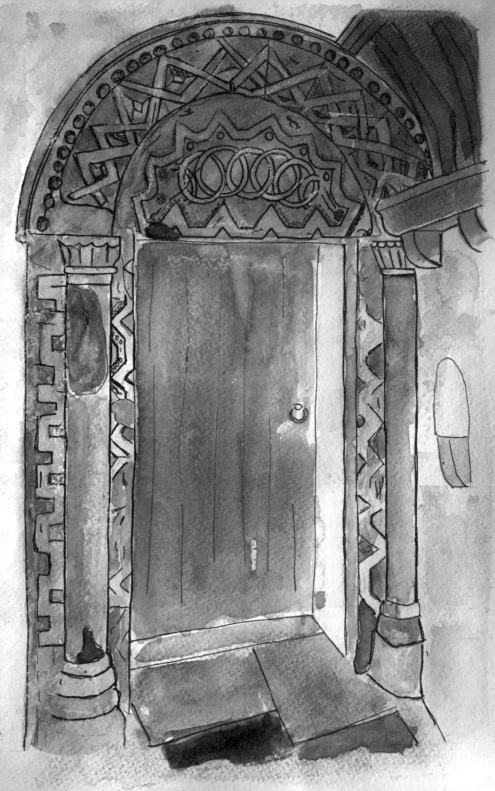

Cury, south door

NN November 2014

Glossary

ABACUS A flat slab forming the uppermost part of a capital.

AGNUS DEI The Lamb of God. In Romanesque sculpture a creature distinguished by its support of a cross.

AMPHISBAENA A serpent or dragon with a second head at the end of its tail.

ANTEFIX An ornamental tile placed at the eaves of a classical building, concealing the jointed tiles of the roof.

APOTROPAIC Having the power to avert evil or deflect misfortune through the use of images, marks, words or gestures.

BABEWYN A medieval term for a grotesque.

BEAKHEAD An ornament in the form of a bird's head, or a human or beast's head, most commonly found superimposed on the roll moulding of an arch.

BLIND A term used to describe a decorative architectural feature which is built into a wall or other masonry, e.g. blind arch, blind arcade.

CAPITAL Topmost part of a column.

CELL A discrete architectural unit e.g. a 'two-cell' church, consisting of a nave and chancel.

CHEVRON The characteristic zigzag decoration found around doorways and windows in Romanesque architecture.

CORBEL A block, often carved, that supports a feature above. A line of corbels is called a corbel table.

CROSSING A central space at the junction of the nave, chancel and transepts.

CUSP A projecting point between the foils in a Gothic arch.

FOIL Lobe formed by the cusping of a circle or an arch. Trefoil, quatrefoil, cinquefoil etc express the number of leaf shapes visible.

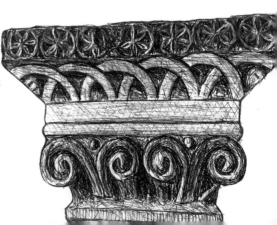

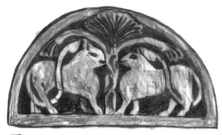

Treneglos

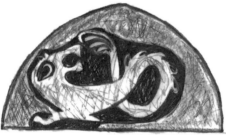

Egloskerry, north door

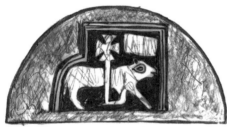

Egloskerry, south door

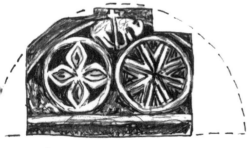

Launceston St Thomas

GOTHIC Architectural style characteristic of the late twelfth to the sixteenth centuries, distinguished by pointed arches, flying buttresses, tracery windows and rib vaulting.

GREEN MAN A head disgorging foliage through the mouth (sometimes also through the eyes and nose) or otherwise growing into leaves, often found carved in architectural sculpture.

HOOD MOULD Projecting moulding above an arch.

IGNEOUS ROCK A rock solidified from lava or magma.

LABEL STOP Ornamental boss at the end of a hood mould.

LINTEL Horizontal stone that bridges an opening such as a doorway.

MAQUETTE A sculptor's preliminary model.

METAMORPHIC ROCK A rock that has undergone transformation by heat and/or pressure.

MISERICORD A bracket (often carved with an image) on the underside of a hinged choir-stall seat, which, when turned up, provided the occupant of the seat with support during long periods of standing.

MOHS SCALE A scale of hardness used in classifying minerals.

OCULUS A round or eye-like opening or design.

OGEE An arch of two 'S' curved mouldings that meet in a pronounced, spike-like point.

ORDER A series of concentric steps receding towards the opening of a doorway or window.

PALMETTE An ornament of radiating petals resembling a palm leaf.

PISCINA A basin for washing ceremonial vessels, usually set in the wall south of an altar.

REREDOS A structure above and behind an altar.

ROOF BOSS A decorative projection that covers the intersection of ribs in a vaulted roof.

ROUNDEL A decorative medallion or disc.

SEDIMENTARY ROCK A rock formed by the deposition of weathered particles of mineral or organic matter on the floor of oceans or other bodies of water.

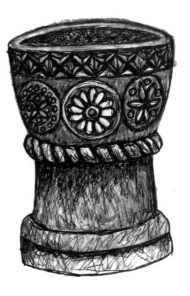

Combeinteignhead 8ᵗʰ August

TYMPANUM The space between the lintel of a doorway and the arch above it.

VOLUTE A spiral scroll.

VOUSSOIR A wedge-shaped stone used in the construction of an arch.

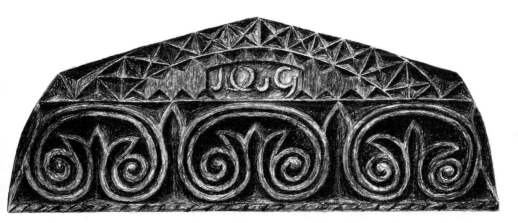

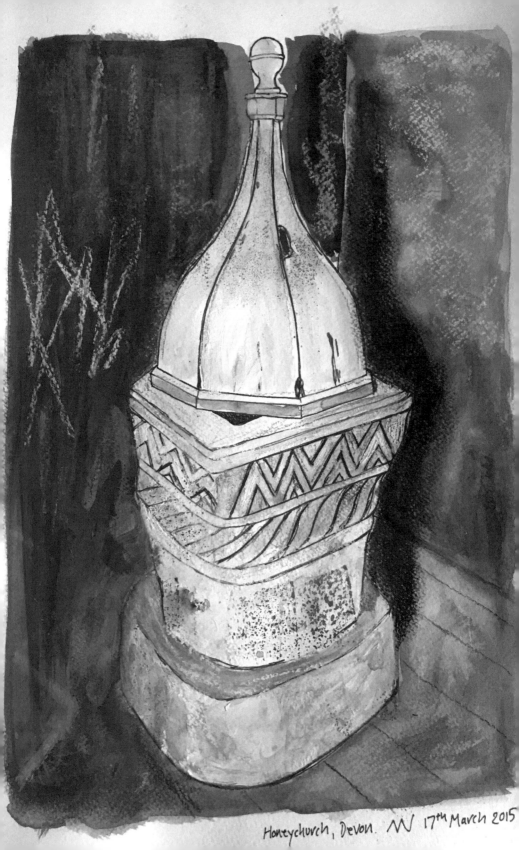

Honeychurch, Devon. ⚒ 17th March 2015

Bibliography

STONES

Anon., 1921. 'Obituary: Mr W. Edmund Sedding', *The Builder*, 4 March, 287 (the initial 'W' is an error).

Cornwall Record Office, 'St Buryan Church, measured and drawn by Edmund Sedding, Architect, Penzance' offprint from *The British Architect*, 23 December 1887.

Godwin, E. W., 1853. 'Notes on Some Examples of Church Architecture in Cornwall', *Archaeological Journal* 10(1): 317–324.

Needleman, C., 1993. *The Work of Craft: An Inquiry into the Nature of Crafts and Craftsmanship*, New York: Knopf.

Pevsner, N., 1951. *The Buildings of England: Cornwall*, London: Penguin.

Rodin, A., 1914. *Cathedrals of France*, London: Country Life.

Sedding, E. H., 1909. *Norman Architecture in Cornwall: A Handbook to Old Cornish Ecclesiastical Sites, with a Note on Manor-Houses*, London: Ward Lock.

Sennett, R., 2009. *The Craftsman*, London: Penguin.

White, K., 1989. *The Bird Path: Collected Longer Poems 1964–1988*, Edinburgh: Mainstream.

Zarnecki, G., 1951. *English Romanesque Sculpture 1066–1140*, London: Tiranti.

Zarnecki, G., 1953. *Later English Romanesque Sculpture 1140–1210*, London: Tiranti.

REDISCOVERING THE ROMANESQUE

Ackroyd, P., 1985 *Hawksmoor*, London, Hamish Hamilton; Ackroyd, P., 1989, *First Light*, London: Abacus.

Caviness, M. H., 1989. 'Broadening the Definitions of "Art": The Reception of Medieval Works in the Context of Post-Impressionist Movements', in P. J. Gallacher and H. Damico (eds.) *Hermeneutics and Medieval Culture*, Albany: State University of New York Press, 259–282.

Mâle, É. 1961 [1913]. *The Gothic Image: Religious Art in France of the Thirteenth Century*, London: Fontana.

Maxwell, R. A., 2006. 'Modern Origins of Romanesque Sculpture' in C. Rudolph (ed.) *A Companion to Medieval Art: Romanesque and Gothic in Northern Europe*, Chichester: Wiley-Blackwell, 334–356.

Perkins, R. A., 2005. 'Devon Architects: Some Notes About Architects, Engineers and Builders etc. Active in Devon Before 1914; A Contribution to Local History and the Study of Building in the County', privately published by the author, Westcountry Studies Library, Exeter, 324–325.

Schapiro, M., 1961. 'Style' in M. Philipson (ed.) *Aesthetics Today*, Clinton, Mass.: World Publishing Co., 81–113.

Swanson, R. N., 1999. *The Twelfth-Century Renaissance*, Manchester: Manchester University Press.

Vallier, D., 1961. *Kunst und Zeugnis*, Zürich: Peter Schifferli.

Walsh, T., 1999. *The Dark Matter of Words: Absence, Unknowing, and Emptiness in Literature*, Carbondale IL: Southern Illinois University Press.

Wilson, H. M., (in press) 'From "Lady Carvers" to Professionals: The Remarkable Pinwill Sisters' Transactions of the Devonshire Association 151.

Woodcock, A., 2005. *Liminal Images: Aspects of Medieval Architectural Sculpture in the South of England from the Eleventh to the Sixteenth Centuries*, British Archaeological Reports, 386, Oxford: John & Erica Hedges.

THE TRENEGLOS LIONS

Alford, S., 1984. 'Romanesque Architectural Sculpture in Dorset: A Selective Catalogue and Commentary', *Proceedings of the Dorset Natural History and Archaeological Society*, 106: 1–22.

Batten, M., 1957. *Stone Sculpture by Direct Carving*, London: Studio Publications.

Beacham, P. and Pevsner, N., 2014. *The Buildings of England: Cornwall*, London: Yale University Press.

Emerson, R. W., 1901. 'Love' in *Essays: First Series*, London: Dent.

Gell, A., 1998. *Art and Agency: An Anthropological Theory*, Oxford: Clarendon Press.

Holdsworth, C., 1991. 'From 1050–1307' in N. Orme (ed.) *Unity and Variety: A History of the Church in Devon and Cornwall*, Exeter Studies in History No. 29, Exeter: University of Exeter Press, 23–52.

Hutton, R., (ed.) 2015 *Physical Evidence for Ritual Acts, Sorcery and Witchcraft in Christian Britain: A Feeling for Magic*, London: Palgrave MacMillan.

Keyser, C. E., 1904. *Norman Tympana and Lintels*, London: Elliot Stock.

Kordecki, L. C., 1980. *Traditions and Development of the Medieval English Dragon*, unpublished PhD thesis, University of Toronto.

Langdon, A. G., 1906. 'Early Christian Monuments' in W. Page (ed.) *The Victoria History of the County of Cornwall*, vol. I, London: Archibald Constable, 407–449.

Loewenthal, L. J. A., 1978. 'Amulets in Medieval Sculpture: I. General Outline', *Folklore* 89: 3–12.

Melinkoff, R., 2004. *Averting Demons: The Protective Power of Medieval Visual Motifs and Themes*, (2 vols), Eugene, Oregon: Wipf & Stock.

Orme, N., 2007. *Cornwall and the Cross: Christianity 500–1560*, Bognor Regis: Phillimore.

Orme, N., 2010. *A History of the County of Cornwall vol. II: Religious History to 1560*, London: The Victoria County History, 32, 201–204.

Preston-Jones, A. and Okasha, E., 2013. *Early Cornish Sculpture*, Corpus of Anglo-Saxon Stone Sculpture XI, Oxford: Oxford University Press.

Solnit, R., 2006. *A Field Guide to Getting Lost*, Edinburgh: Canongate.

Tyerman, C., 1996. *Who's Who in Early Medieval England*, London: Shepheard Walwyn.

Wood, R., 1997. 'The Two Lions at Milborne Port', *Somerset Archaeology and Natural History* 141: 1–15.

Zarnecki, G., 1992. 'English Romanesque Art 1066–1200: Sculpture' in G. Zarnecki, *Further Studies in Romanesque Sculpture*, London: Pindar.

A LINE IN THE CLIFF

Bristow, C. M., 2001, 'Some Notable Cornish Building and Decorative Stones', *Geoscience in Southwest England* 10: 223–229.

King, A., 2011. *Strategic Stone Study: A Building Stone Atlas of Cornwall and the Isles of Scilly*, London: English Heritage, 12.

Masey, P. E., 1882. *Observations on Beer Stone*, Exeter: James Townsend, 4.

Reid, C., Barrow, G. and Dewey H., 1910. *The Geology of the Country around Padstow and Camelford*, Geological Survey of Great Britain, Sheet Memoir 335–336, London: HMSO, 91.

Robson, J., 1964. 'The Cornish "Greenstones"' in K. F. G. Hosking and G. J. Shrimpton (eds) *Present Views of Some Aspects of the Geology of Cornwall and Devon*, Penzance: Royal Geological Society of Cornwall, 115–130.

Stanier, P., 2015. *South West Stone Quarries: Building Stone Quarries in the West of England*, Truro: Twelveheads Press.

IN ZIGZAG SHADOW

Baxter, R., 2004: 'Beakhead Ornament and the Corpus of Romanesque Sculpture', *Historic Churches* 11: 8–10.

Crawford, M., 2009. *The Case for Working with Your Hands: Or Why Office Work is Bad for Us and Fixing Things Feels Good*, London: Viking.

Dew, R., 1926. *A History of the Parish and Church of Kilkhampton*, London: Wells Gardner Darton.

Halliday, F. E., 2001 [1959]. *A History of Cornwall*, 2nd edition, Thirsk: House of Stratus.

Hervey, J., 1815. *Meditations and Contemplations*, London: Richard Evans.

Hill, P., 2014. 'William Arnold and his Stonemasons', *Somerset and Dorset Notes and Queries* 37: 317–324.

Moss, R., 2009. *Romanesque Chevron Ornament: The Language of British, Norman and Irish Sculpture in the Twelfth Century*, British Archaeological Reports International Series 1908, Oxford: Archaeopress.

Needleman, C., 1993. *The Work of Craft: An Inquiry into the Nature of Crafts and Craftsmanship*, London: Kodansha.

Thurlby, M., 1991. 'The Romanesque Cathedral circa 1114–1200' in Michael Swanton (ed.) *Exeter Cathedral: A Celebration*, Exeter: Dean and Chapter, 37–45.

Treves, F., 1935. *Highways and Byways in Dorset*, London: Macmillan.

Woodcock, A., 2013. *Of Sirens and Centaurs: Medieval Sculpture at Exeter Cathedral*, Exeter: Impress.

Woodcock, A., 2017 'The Romanesque Sculpture of North Devon and North Cornwall', *Devon Buildings Group Newsletter* 35: 13–30.

BEAKHEADS AT MORWENSTOW

Chope, R. P., 1940. *The Book of Hartland*, Torquay: Devonshire Press.

Clarke, K. M., 1920. 'Norman Corbels at Plympton', *Devon and Cornwall Notes and Queries* 11: 1–2.

Deacon, B. and Payton, P., 1993. 'Re-inventing Cornwall: Culture Change on the European Periphery', *Cornish Studies* (2nd ser.) 1: 62–79.

Farquharson, G., 2005. *Clan Farquharson: A History*, Stroud: Tempus.

Henry, F. and Zarnecki, G., 1957. 'Romanesque Arches Decorated with Human and Animal Heads', *Journal of the British Archaeological Association*, 3rd series, 20, 1–34.

Hockin, J. R. A., 1949. *Walking in Cornwall*, London: Methuen (4th ed.).

Jenkins, S., 1999. *England's Thousand Best Churches*, London: Penguin.

Mee, A. (ed.), 1937. *Cornwall: England's Farthest South*, London: Hodder and Stoughton.

Murphy, S., 2005. *Stone Mad*, Cork: Collins Press.

Rhodes, C., 1994. *Primitivism and Modern Art*, London: Thames & Hudson.

Slader, J. M., 1968. *The Churches of Devon*, Newton Abbot: David & Charles.

West, J. K. 1982. 'Two Romanesque Stone Carvings' in R. A. Higham, J. P. Allan and S. R. Blaylock 'Excavations at Okehampton Castle, Devon; Part 2, the Bailey', *Proceedings of the Devon Archaeological Society* 40: 79–82.

Woodcock, A., 2015. 'Reconsidering the Romanesque Sculpture of Cornwall', *Journal of the Royal Institution of Cornwall*, 57–72.

FOUR FONTS

Andrew, S., 2011. Late Medieval Roof Bosses in the Churches of Devon, unpublished PhD thesis, University of Plymouth.

Anon., 1926. 'Obituary – Miss Kate Marie Clarke', *Transactions of the Devonshire Association* 57: 26–27.

Camille, M., 1992. *Image on the Edge: The Margins of Medieval Art*, London: Reaktion.

Camille, M., 1993. 'Mouths and Meanings: Towards an Anti-Iconography of Medieval Art' in B. Cassidy (ed.) *Iconography at the Crossroads*, Princeton University: Department of Art and Archaeology, 43–58.

Census Returns of England and Wales, 1861. Kew, Surrey, England: The National Archives of the UK (TNA): Public Record Office (PRO), 1861, Class: RG 9; Piece: 1594; Folio: 25; Page: 3; GSU roll: 542837.

Cherry, B. and Pevsner, N. 1991. *The Buildings of England: Devon*, London: Yale.

Clarke, K. M., 1904. 'The Conventual Houses of Exeter and the Neighbourhood', *Devon Notes and Queries* 3: 129–151.

Clarke, K. M., 1913. 'The Luppitt Font', *Devon and Cornwall Notes and Queries* 7: 201–205.

Clarke, K. M., 1906. 'The Symbolism of the Ancient Fonts of Stoke Canon, St Marychurch, and Alphington', *Devon and Cornwall Notes and Queries* 4: 129–139.

Clarke, K. M., 1913–22. 'The Baptismal Fonts of Devon', *Transactions of the Devonshire Association* I (1913) 45: 314–29; II (1914) 46: 428–36; III (1915) 47: 349–56; IV (1916) 48: 302–19; V (1918) 50: 583–87; VI (1919) 51: 211–21; VII (1920) 52: 327–35; VIII (1921) 53: 226–31; IX (1922) 54: 216–23.

Corser, C., 1980. A Catalogue of Norman Fonts in Devon, 5 vols., unpublished MPhil thesis, University of Exeter School of English.

Cresswell, B. F. C. A. G., 1904–1912. Drawings of 150 Devon Fonts, Devon Heritage Centre, Sowton.

Druce, G. C., 1919. 'The Elephant in Medieval Legend and Art', *Journal of the Royal Archaeological Institute* 76: 3–70.

Gardner, A., 1935. *A Handbook of English Medieval Sculpture*, Cambridge: Cambridge University Press.

Hoskins, W. G., 1954. *A New Survey of England: Devon*, London: Collins.

Jarrett, M. J. M. and Strevens, B., 2010. *Out of Dunkeswell: US Navy Fleet Air Wing 7 and 479th Antisubmarine Group USAF*, Honiton: Southwest Airfields Heritage Trust.

Mâle, É., 1978 [1922]. *Religious Art in France: The Twelfth Century. A Study of the Origins of Medieval Iconography*, Princeton University Press.

Yapp, W. B., 1987. 'The Iconography of the Font at Toller Fratrum', *Proceedings of the Dorset Natural History and Archaeological Society* 109: 1–4.

THE BEASTS OF BODMIN

Anderson, M. D., 1938. *Animal Carvings in British Churches*, Cambridge: Cambridge University Press.

Fryer, A. C., 1901. 'A Group of Transitional-Norman Fonts (North-East Cornwall)', *Journal of the British Archaeological Association* 7: 215–218.

Martin, M., 1978. *A Wayward Genius: Neville Northy Burnard, Cornish Sculptor 1818–1878*, Padstow: Lodenek Press.

Norway, A. H., 1923. *Highways and Byways in Devon and Cornwall*, London: Macmillan.

Turner, E., 1867. 'The Lost Towns of Northeye and Hydneye', *Sussex Archaeological Collections* 19: 1–35.

CATHEDRAL STONEMASON

Bishop, H. E., 1935. 'Montacute Corbel: The Western Corbels of the Choir', *Friends of Exeter Cathedral Fifth Annual Report 1934*, 11–13.

Cave, C. J. P., 1953. *Medieval Carvings in Exeter Cathedral*, London: Penguin.

Clarke, K. M., 1920. 'Norman Corbels at Plympton', *Devon and Cornwall Notes and Queries* 11: 1–2.

Coldstream, N., 1991. *Medieval Craftsmen: Masons and Sculptors*, London: British Museum Press.

Erskine, A. M., 1983 (ed. and trans.) *The Accounts of the Fabric of Exeter Cathedral, 1279–1353: Part I 1279–1326*, Torquay: Devon and Cornwall Record Society new series vol. 24.

Givens, J., 1991. 'The Fabric Accounts of Exeter Cathedral as a Record of Medieval Sculptural Practice', *Gesta* 30: 112–118.

Harpham, G. G., 1982. *On the Grotesque: Strategies of Contradiction in Art and Literature*, Princeton, New Jersey: Princeton University Press.

Henderson, C., 1964 [1925]. *The Cornish Church Guide and Parochial History of Cornwall*, Truro: Bradford Barton.

Langdon, Arthur G., 1906. 'Early Christian Monuments' in W. Page (ed.) *The Victoria History of the County of Cornwall*, vol. I, London: Archibald Constable, 407–449.

Maccoll, D. S., 1905. 'Grania in Church: Or the Clever Daughter', *Burlington Magazine* 8: 80–86.

Pevsner, N., 1953. 'A Note on the Art of the Exeter Carvers' in C. J. P. Cave *Medieval Carvings in Exeter Cathedral*, London: Penguin, 25–32.

Prideaux, E. K. and Shafto, G. R. H., 1910. *Bosses and Corbels of Exeter Cathedral: An Illustrated Study in Decorative and Symbolic Design*, Exeter: James G. Commin.

Swanton, M., 1979. *Roof-Bosses and Corbels of Exeter Cathedral*, Exeter: Dean and Chapter.

Woodcock, A., 2017. 'Beasts and Beakheads: Romanesque Sculpture at Morwenstow', in P. Holden (ed.) *Celebrating Pevsner: New Research on Cornish Architecture*, London: Francis Boutle, 41–48.

Yates, W., 1997. 'An Introduction to the Grotesque: Theoretical and Theological Considerations' in J. L. Adams and W. Yates (eds.) *The Grotesque in Art and Literature: Theological Reflections*, Michigan and Cambridge: W. B. Eerdmans, 1–68.

Ziolkowski, J. M., 2008. *Solomon and Marcolf*, Cambridge Mass.: Harvard University Press.

CHURCH OF THE STORMS

Anon., 1808. 'North Porch of East Teignmouth Church, Devonshire', *Antiquarian and Topographical Cabinet* III, 1–2.

Cummings, A. H., 1875. *Churches and Antiquities of Cury and Gunwalloe in the Lizard District Including Local Traditions*, London: Marlborough & Co.

Drake, C. S., 2003. *The Romanesque Fonts of Northern Europe and Scandinavia*, Woodbridge, Suffolk: Boydell.

Frost, R. O. and Steketee, G., 2010. *Stuff: Compulsive Hoarding and the Meaning of Things*, New York: Mariner Books.

Hoban, R., 2001. *Amaryllis Night and Day*, London: Bloomsbury.

Rawson, P., 1984. *Ceramics*, Philadelphia: University of Pennsylvania Press.

Woodcock, A. 2009. 'Honeysuckle and Red Sandstone: Some Characteristics of Romanesque Stonecarving in South Devon', *Transactions of the Devonshire Association* 141: 77–92.

Woodcock, A., 2016. 'A Stone "Richly Embossed with Volutes": The Romanesque Tympanum from East Teignmouth', *Transactions of the Devonshire Association* 148: 293–310.

BIRD MAN

Anon., 1937 (January). 'Obituary: P. M. Johnston', *Journal of the Royal Institute of British Architects*, 305.

Bonner, Arthur, 1937. 'In Memoriam, Philip Mainwaring Johnston', *Surrey Archaeological Collections*, 45: 168–169.

Crow, J., 'Philip Mainwaring Johnston (1865–1936)', *Biographies of the Founding Fathers of the Archaeological Society and Other Members of Note*, unpublished notes and ephemera, Sussex Archaeological Society Library, Lewes.

De Silvey, C., 2006. 'Observed Decay: Telling Stories with Mutable Things', *Journal of Material Culture* 11(3): 318–338.

F. B. S., 1937. 'Obituary: Philip M. Johnston', *Sussex Notes and Queries* 6: 152–153.

Harbison, R., 2015. *Ruins and Fragments: Tales of Loss and Rediscovery*, London: Reaktion.

Johnston, P. M., 1927. 'Bishopsteignton Church', *Journal of the British Archaeological Association* 33: 99–122.

Johnston, P. M., 1937. 'Reminiscentia', *Journal of the Royal Institute of British Architects*, 355–356.

Pickard-Cambridge, O., 1891. 'On New and Rare Spiders found in 1889 and 1890', *Proceedings of the Dorset Natural History and Antiquarian Field Club* 12: 80–98.

Salzman, L. F., 1946. 'A History of the Sussex Archaeological Society', *Sussex Archaeological Collections* 85: 1–76.

Van Der Hoorn, M., 2003. 'Exorcizing Remains: Architectural Fragments as Intermediaries between History and Individual Experience', *Journal of Material Culture* 8: 189–213.

HONEYCHURCH TWILIGHT

Bynum, C. W., 1997. 'Wonder', *American Historical Review* 102: 1–26.

Carruthers, M., 1998. *The Craft of Thought: Meditation, Rhetoric, and the Making of Images*, Cambridge: Cambridge University Press, 82–87.

Costello, Hilary, 2006. *Sky-Blue is the Sapphire, Crimson the Rose: Stillpoint of Desire in John of Forde*, Kalamazoo: Cistercian Publications.

Marder, M., 2016. *Dust*, London: Bloomsbury.

Rudolph, C., 1990. *The "Things of Greater Importance": Bernard of Clairvaux's Apologia and the Medieval Attitude Toward Art*, Philadelphia: University of Pennsylvania Press.

Schapiro, M. 1977 [1947] 'On the Aesthetic Attitude in Romanesque Art' in *Romanesque Art*, London: Chatto and Windus, 1–27.

Williams, D., 1996. *Deformed Discourse: The Function of the Monster in Medieval Thought and Literature*, Exeter: Exeter University Press.

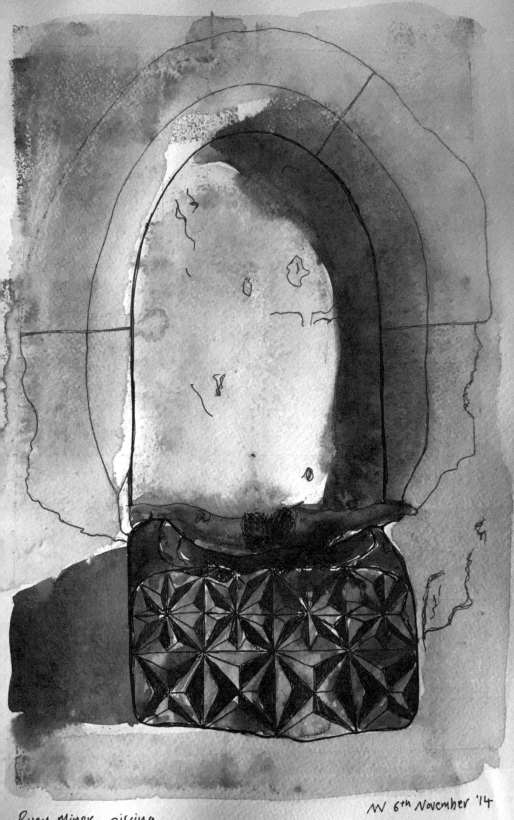

Ruan Minor, piscina

WW 6th November '14

Acknowledgements

My heartfelt thanks to everyone who believed in this project and supported it in one way or another over the last four years, by offering practical help, financial help, raw enthusiasm, teaching me to write better, coming on field trips, sending me books, reading early drafts, making lunch, taking photos, asking awkward questions, drinking tea, offering suggestions, disliking it, liking it, having a laugh, pointing me in directions I hadn't considered, and in a million other ways – it is because of you that it was possible, and because of you that I kept going:

Dr John Allan, Madeleine Amos, Glyn Antle-Trapnell, Jay & Scott Armstrong, Tom Beattie, Dr Stuart Blaylock, Matt Borne, Laura Clarke, Gracie & Adrian Cooper, Cornish Buildings Group, Cornwall Heritage Trust, Cornwall Historic Churches Trust, Tanya Covi, Dr Simon Crook, Chris Daniels, Drift Records, Paul Dodgson, Pip Dunwell, Rob Escot, Exeter Cathedral, Friends of Hugh Miller, John Goodliffe, Dr Tom Goskar, Malcolm Green, Polly Jean Harvey, Matt Hoskins, Corella Hughes, Impress Books, Julith Jedamus, Mark Jervis, Louise Kenward, Paul Kingsnorth, Ed Kluz, Damian Lawrence, Little Toller Books, Brett Long, Lynne Mably, Susy Marriott, Dr Jo Mattingly, Joe Milne, The Minack (Derek & Jeannie Tangye) Trust, Moniack Mhor, Gary Morley, Richard Mortimer, The Morrab Library, Music's Not Dead, Dr Theresa Oakley, Richard Parker, Jane Pugh, The 'Q' Fund (Sir Arthur Quiller Couch Memorial Fund), Del Querns, Mimi Rousell, Royal Cornwall Museum, Charlotte Sabin, Chris Sampson, Tom Scott, Helen Shipman, Society of Antiquaries, Jay St John Knight, Anna & Marc Steinmetzer, Sussex Archaeological Society, Totnes Bookshop, Laurence de Vaz, Dr Jayne Wackett, Diane Walker, Mark Ware, Owen Whitfield, Marcus Williamson, Dr Richard Willis, Dr Helen Wilson, Ann & Alan Woodcock, Jennifer Woodcock, Jon Woolcott, Rich Wortley.

Last but by no means least, here's to the eleventh- and twelfth-century stonemasons whose work lives on.

A.W.
2019

Little Toller Books

Anthology and Biography
ARBOREAL: WOODLAND WORDS
CORNERSTONES: SUBTERRANEAN STORIES
MY HOUSE OF SKY: THE LIFE OF J.A. BAKER

Field Notes
DEER ISLAND *Neil Ansell*
ORISON FOR A CURLEW *Horatio Clare*
SOMETHING OF HIS ART *Horatio Clare*
ON THE MARSHES *Carol Donaldson*
THE TREE *John Fowles*
SAVAGE GODS *Paul Kingsnorth*
LOVE, MADNESS, FISHING *Dexter Petley*
WATER AND SKY *Neil Sentance*
RIDGE AND FURROW *Neil Sentance*
KING OF DUST *Alex Woodcock*

Monographs
HAVERGEY *John Burnside*
LANDFILL *Tim Dee*
HERBACEOUS *Paul Evans*
EAGLE COUNTRY *Seán Lysaght*
SPIRITS OF PLACE *Sara Maitland*
MERMAIDS *Sophia Kingshill*
LIMESTONE COUNTRY *Fiona Sampson*
SNOW *Marcus Sedgwick*
BLACK APPLES OF GOWER *Iain Sinclair*
BEYOND THE FELL WALL *Richard Skelton*
SHARKS *Martha Sprackland*
ON SILBURY HILL *Adam Thorpe*

The Oliver Rackham Library
THE ASH TREE *Oliver Rackham*
THE ANCIENT WOODS OF THE HELFORD RIVER *Oliver Rackham*
THE ANCIENT WOODS OF SOUTH EAST WALES *Oliver Rackham*

Nature Classics
THROUGH THE WOODS *H.E. Bates*
MEN AND THE FIELDS *Adrian Bell*
THE MIRROR OF THE SEA *Joseph Conrad*
ISLAND YEARS, ISLAND FARM *Frank Fraser Darling*
THE MAKING OF THE ENGLISH LANDSCAPE *W.G. Hoskins*
THE PATTERN UNDER THE PLOUGH *George Ewart Evans*
A SHEPHERD'S LIFE *W.H. Hudson*
FOUR HEDGES *Clare Leighton*
DREAM ISLAND *R.M. Lockley*
THE UNOFFICIAL COUNTRYSIDE *Richard Mabey*
RING OF BRIGHT WATER *Gavin Maxwell*
IN PURSUIT OF SPRING *Edward Thomas*
THE NATURAL HISTORY OF SELBORNE *Gilbert White*

LOWER DAIRY, TOLLER FRATRUM, DORSET
W. littletoller.co.uk E. books@littletoller.co.uk

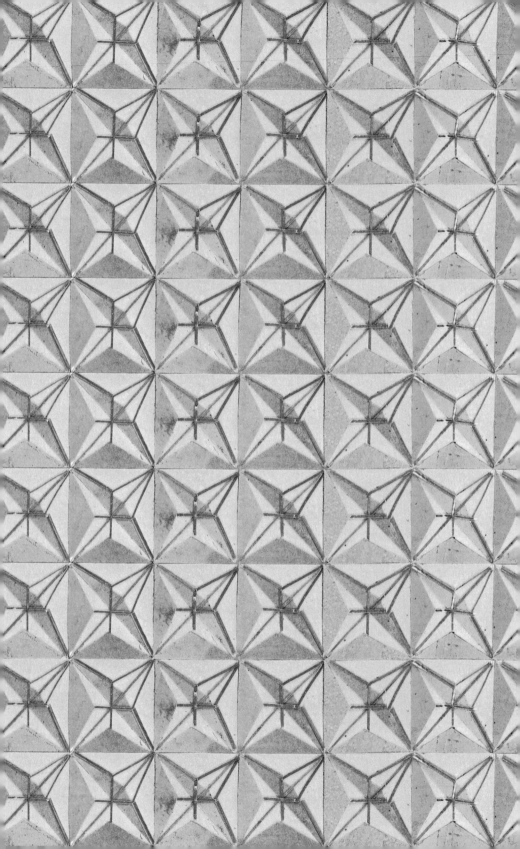